The WA State Emergency Service (SES)

History from Civil Defence into the 21st Century

Gordon M Hall ESM

Copyright © Gordon M Hall
Published: 2021 by
Leschenault Press

ISBN: 978-0-648832690 – Paperback Edition
ISBN: 978-0-648949695 – E-Book Edition

All rights reserved.

The right of Gordon M Hall to be identified as author of this Work has been asserted by him in accordance with sections 77 and 78 of the Copyright, Designs and Patents Act 1988.

No part of this publication may be reproduced, stored in retrieval system, copied in any form or by any means, electronic, mechanical, photocopying, recording or otherwise transmitted without written permission from the publisher. You must not circulate this book in any format.

All source material has been fully acknowledged and used with permissions where applicable. Should you feel any material within is in breach of copyright please contact the publisher in the first instance.

Cover Design by Luke Buxton | www.lukebuxton.com

Table of Contents

Foreword by the Minister for Emergency Services i
Foreword by the Fire and Emergency Services Commissioner iii
Introduction v
Chapter 1 - Overview 1
Chapter 2 - Civil Defence 3
Chapter 3 - The WA SES – 1959 to 1999 25
Chapter 4 - Volunteer Representation 53
Chapter 5 - Emergency Services Levy 69
Chapter 6 - Australian Awards for Outstanding Service 72
Chapter 7 - State Awards for Outstanding Service 79
Chapter 8 - Lives Lost During Active Service 85
Chapter 9 - The Bunker 92
Chapter 10 - Publications 99
Chapter 11 - Training 104
Chapter 12 - Uniforms and Insignias 110
Chapter 13 - Major Awards and Achievements 117
Chapter 14 - Education and Heritage Centre 124
Chapter 15 - Other information and Stories 127
Chapter 16 - Significant Operations or Events 133
Chapter 17 - History of Some SES Units 157
Acknowledgements 209
Biographies 210

Foreword by the Minister for Emergency Services

For more than 70 years, the Western Australian State Emergency Service has served as a beacon of light for those in their time of need. The rich history of the State Emergency Service and the natural disasters that defined its role in the Western Australian community are captured in this book.

This comprehensive account is a reminder of how incredibly fortunate this State is to have thousands of volunteers who are passionate about keeping their community safe. The State Emergency Service is also testament to the strength of volunteerism in Western Australia.

In a State as vast as Western Australia, our emergency services would not function without dedicated volunteers like those in the State Emergency Service. Tens of thousands of hours are dedicated every year by a legion of proud and dedicated State Emergency Service volunteers who go above and beyond the call of duty.

The events recounted in this book also highlight the time State Emergency Service volunteers sacrifice being away from their families, friends and workplaces in their altruistic pursuit of helping others. The State Government recognises this commitment, as well as the huge wealth of knowledge and skills within emergency services, with better recognition and support for volunteers being a key priority.

As Emergency Services Minister, I have worked diligently to ensure the State Emergency Service is adequately funded and resourced to empower and equip local volunteers to support their communities.

I congratulate all those involved in this book and their work to preserve the story of the State Emergency Service for generations to come.

The Honourable Francis Logan MLA
Minister for Emergency Services

Foreword by the
Fire and Emergency Services Commissioner

In Australia, the orange coloured uniform is synonymous with the State Emergency Service. However, the history of the service, and those in its orange overalls, is broadly unknown to many in the community. From its beginnings as the Civil Defence, the State Emergency Service has flourished into a modern, professional and dynamic service.

This book serves as an important and thorough account of the Western Australian State Emergency Service and the critical role it has played during significant natural disasters.

Home to the most cyclone prone area in Australia, the Western Australian coastline between Broome and Exmouth has seen its fair share of destructive weather events. Further, in the south and inland areas, floods, earthquakes and severe storms have all made their mark on different corners of the State over the past 70 years. This is in addition to the hundreds of search-and-rescue missions undertaken by the State Emergency Service each year, often in harsh and unforgiving terrain.

Among the devastation of these incidents are stories of bravery and dedication of State Emergency Service volunteers helping their communities through tough times. There is a deep gratitude from those they assist and recent initiatives such as Wear Orange Wednesday (WOW Day) help to echo these thanks.

The work of the State Emergency Service goes beyond its combat role in responding to incidents. Through community engagement and education, the

State Emergency Service has helped build stronger communities who are more resilient when natural disasters strike.

The State Emergency Service family is a strong one whose diverse volunteers come from every walk of life. In 2020, Western Australia is fortunate to have over 2,100 State Emergency Service volunteers, located from Kununurra in the north of the State to Esperance in the south.

This book is testament to the commitment and enthusiasm of those volunteers and will help to preserve the history of the service as it continues to grow in the 21st Century.

Darren Klemm AFSM
Fire and Emergency Services Commissioner

Introduction

The compilation of the history of the State Emergency Service (SES) in Western Australia is intended to bring together that which is known by so many but often not written and that which was learned through research; all of which led to the formation and development of the SES in Western Australia. It covers the subsequent years, from when it was part of the Civil Defence and Emergency Service of Western Australia, part of the Police Department, its' own entity as the WA State Emergency Service and in more recent years as a service under the general responsibility of the Department of Fire and Emergency Services.

In the years tracing the history of the SES, many past and present SES Volunteers and Staff were able to provide pieces of information, including old Civil Defence memorabilia that was being discarded.

By 1998 there were more than eighty State Emergency Service units established throughout the state as a follow on from the early Civil Defence groups in Western Australia. Today there are sixty-five SES units based across the state.

The writing of this book has been made possible by the assistance of two peer reviewers, John Capes OAM and Allen Gale, as well as proof reading by Kaye Lawry and Kerry Hall.

The publication was made possible by the support of the Minister for Emergency Services, Fran Logan MLA, and the Fire and Emergency Services Commissioner, Darren Klemm AFSM.

To all the SES Volunteers, both past and present, the community greatly appreciates your assistance and thank you for always being there.

Chapter 1 - Overview

Western Australia is threatened with many natural disasters including cyclones, floods, tsunami, storms, earthquakes and bushfires. All of these represent a threat to life and property.

The Australian Constitution gives responsibility for natural hazards to the State jurisdictions. However, the Commonwealth Government has provided some support and guidance through the Civil Defence and other organisations.

At a state jurisdictional level, the responsibility has not always been clearly defined.

Over the years the roles have moved from one organisation to another, both at a State and Commonwealth Government level.

In Western Australia, there were many years when there was no legislation covering these natural disasters. There was uncertainty within the command structures along with a lack of legal authority for emergency management agencies to take appropriate action.

Until 2005, Western Australia was the only state in Australia that did not have emergency management legislation covering its response to these disasters.

The *FESA Act (1998)* covered the structure and responsibilities, however, still did not give any legal coverage for emergency management for the State Emergency Service Volunteers in their Hazard Management Agency (HMA) response roles for cyclones, floods, tsunami, storms and earthquakes.

The History of the WA SES sets out the timeline from Civil Defence to SES and the subsequent fire and emergency agencies under which the SES Volunteers operated.

It also attempts to cover some of the support roles undertaken by the SES as well as several interesting operations.

It is well recognised by communities and all levels of government that the altruistic nature of State Emergency Service Volunteers provides significant social capital by instilling a sense of community and caring, a level of civic pride, and a sense of self-reliance and security for their own community.

This model of volunteerism for the State Emergency Service provides the Volunteers with a great sense of achievement and community belonging, although at times they may feel undervalued when changes are made without consultation and an assumption that they will always respond to an emergency regardless of circumstances.

Change within the SES is constant and very often led by Government or State politics. A considerable amount of time and resources are dedicated by Volunteers to keep up with these constant changes in training, command organisations and the general requirements and demands by the parent body and their communities.

WA SES Roundel in the state colours with the black Swan in the middle (photo courtesy DFES)

Chapter 2 - Civil Defence

There was a long lead up to the formation of the State Emergency Service in Western Australia, involving both the Commonwealth and State Government over a number of years and was based on the provision of a Civil Defence role for Australia by the State jurisdictions.

The Commonwealth Government was heavily involved with the State jurisdictions, providing guidance and resources over many years.

In a ministerial statement in 1959, then federal Minister for the Interior, Gordon Freeth, stated,

> *"It is a basic principle that the States are responsible for the development of their own Civil Defence planning and programs with the Commonwealth providing national guidance and coordination as necessary"*

This principle remains the basis of the Commonwealth Government's involvement in Civil Defence.

During this period 1936 – 1966 all State Governments and Territories established Civil Defence Directorates. Over that period, it was considered that these organisations were little more than planning and coordinating headquarters with a limited and ill-defined role in the event of a disaster.

There was considerable variation between the States in the way they set up for Civil Defence.

A brief chronological overview of the events relating to Civil Defence is detailed below.

<u>1936</u>

In 1936 a Commonwealth and State Government ministerial conference was held in Adelaide where it was agreed that each State should be responsible for protecting their population against gas attack along with training personnel for essential Civil Defence services.

To supplement State efforts, the Commonwealth agreed to train key personnel and provide equipment, manuals, technical information and key advice.

There was no formal agreement at this stage between State jurisdictions and the Commonwealth Government relating to areas of responsibility.

Most of the Civil Defence work was handled by different Commonwealth Government departments.

1939

In 1939 the Department of Defence was appointed as the co-ordinating authority for national defence plans.

Following the Commonwealth/State Conference of 31 March 1939, a Directorate of Civilian Defence and State Co-operation, within the Department of Defence Co-ordination, was established to handle Civil Defence and State co-operation matters.

This Directorate was the authority for national air raid precaution activities and dealing with State works of defence value. The OIC of the Directorate corresponded directly with each State's responsible officer regarding technical matters and the execution of agreed policies including arranging for these Federal and State officers to meet in direct conference regarding the preparation of defence plans.

Col R.M.W Thirkell MBE VD was the Director of Civilian Defence and State Co-operation from 1940 until the Directorate was abolished on 26 June 1941.

1941

With the growth of Civil Defence Organisations and the general development of Civil Defence measures, a separate Commonwealth Department under separate Ministerial direction was established on 26 June 1941.

The Directorate was thereafter administered by the newly formed Department of Home Security that had the following responsibilities:

1. Acting in an advisory and co-ordinating capacity in relation to the government of the states in the measures for the protection

of the lives and property of the civilian population in the event of an emergency arising out of the war;
2. Compensation for Civil Defence workers and the dependants of personnel who suffered injuries while on duty or whilst training; and for injuries sustained while carrying out essential duties during periods of enemy action;
3. Protection of bulk oil installations by screen walling, bunding and precautionary fire measures;
4. Preparation of schemes and supervision of their implementation to meet the requirements of the services, along with preparation of technical bulletins and posters illustrating the need for camouflage measures to protect vital installations and to protect vital equipment;
5. Prohibition of work near aerodromes under National Security (Supplementary) Regulation No 58;
6. Securing appropriate measure of uniformity in essential codes with regards to lighting of vehicles, air raid warnings and shelter facilities;
7. Air raid precaution measures in respect of Commonwealth establishments;
8. Financial arrangements between Commonwealth and State governments in connection with Civil Defence matters; and
9. Securing firefighting equipment, steel helmets, respirators and other essential equipment for the Commonwealth and for distribution to the states.

Other responsibilities of the Department of Home Security in Civil Defence matters included:

1. Establishment of schools for air raid precautions training;
2. Furnishing technical advice to the state and Commonwealth departments;
3. Conducting research and experiments;
4. Preparation, printing and distribution of standard textbooks; and
5. Distribution of films.

In 1945 the functions of the Department of Home Security were extended to include the administration of the following:

1. National Security Regulations;
2. National Security (General) Regulations;
3. National Security (Civil Defence Workers' Compensation) Regulations;
4. National Security (Supplementary) Regulations No 58;
5. National Security (Camouflage) Regulations; and
6. National Security (Protection of Bulk Oil Installations) Regulations.

The work of the Department of Home Security was closely related to wartime activities and was a vital national necessity in the early months of the war with Japan. At its peak in 1943 the department employed 183 staff; however, as the war moved away from the shores of Australia, the department declined in importance.

During the vital stages of establishing the Department of Home Security, the Secretary of the Department was also the Secretary of the Department of Defence, but later the Assistant Secretary, Mr A.W. Welch became Secretary. Around the same time, Professor W.J. Dakin was appointed Technical Director (Camouflage). Shortly later, the National Security (Camouflage) Regulations were promulgated under which control over camouflage was vested in the Defence Central Camouflage Committee administered by the Department of Home Security.

Rapid extension of Service Requirements following Japan's entry into the war necessitated the establishment of an expanded camouflage organisation to cope with these growing demands.

1942

A Research and Experiments Section was established in the Department of Home Security in March 1942. Around this time, a Scientific Advisory Committee was established, and liaison channels were opened up between Great Britain, the United States, Russia, and other countries through which technical information was received in this country.

1943

In January 1943, a Training and Inspection Section was established in the Department of Home Security with an advanced course for Instructors from the State Civil Defence Organisations conducted by the Department in Melbourne. This was followed by tests of the Civil Defence arrangements in Hobart, in the Queensland coastal towns and in the Perth-Fremantle areas.

1944

From April 1944 onwards Civil Defence policy was reviewed on a number of occasions and restrictions were gradually relaxed.

1945

In June 1945, a report was issued by the Committee of Review into the Civil Staffing of Wartime Activities determining that the Department of Home Security was responsible for the following matters:

1. the recovery and disposal of equipment, some of which is Government property and some of which was secured under Lend-Lease;
2. the administration of the financial agreement between the Commonwealth and the states in regard to Civil Defence measures;
3. the administration of National Security Regulations referred to in paragraph 5 above;
4. the compilation of the history of the department's activities;
5. camouflage research;
6. the preparation of detailed proposals for a nucleus Civil Defence organisation; and
7. the compilation of a departmental war book and chapters in the Commonwealth War Book relating to Civil Defence measures.

In November 1945, on the advice of the Defence Committee, War Cabinet resolved that:

1. there was no longer any necessity to maintain Civil Defence organisations on a reserve basis;
2. the nucleus Civil Defence organisation in the post war period should be limited to a planning organisation;

3. the Commonwealth should set up a planning organisation to keep state planning organisations advised on Civil Defence matters and to co-ordinate all state Civil Defence plans.

1946

On 1 February 1946, the Department of Home Security was abolished, and the Department of the Interior absorbed its activities.

This was notified in Commonwealth Gazette No 23 of 7 February 1946.

The following persons were appointed by the Commonwealth Government to the position of Minister for Home Security:

Hon Joseph Palmer Abbott - June 1941 to October 1941

Hon Hubert Peter Lazzarini - October 1941 to February 1946

The following persons were appointed by the Commonwealth Government to the position of Secretary:

Sir F.G. Shedden July - 1941 to December 1941

A.W. Welch July - 1942 to March 1944

M.S. Thomson March - 1944 to July 1945

W.N.C. Fairweather of the Department of Defence acted as Secretary from 25 July 1945 to February 1946.

1955

In February 1955 the full brunt of a La Nina weather pattern affected the central NSW area, which resulted in severe flooding of a number of places including the severe flooding of the entire Murray-Darling river system.

Many lives were lost and more than 7000 buildings and homes were damaged.

As a result of this disaster, the States of NSW and Victoria commenced the formation of State Emergency Service Units.

Severe flooding was also experienced in the Avon Valley in WA.

1959

In a ministerial statement in 1959, Interior Minister Gordon Freeth said,

> *"It is a basic principle that the States are responsible for the development of their own Civil Defence planning and programs with the Commonwealth providing national guidance and coordination as necessary".*

This principle has never been challenged and remains the basis of the Commonwealth Government's involvement in Civil Defence.

WA Civil Defence Volunteers training – circa 1960s

(photo courtesy DFES)

WA Civil Defence Volunteers training – circa 1960s

(photo courtesy DFES)

1966

The Commonwealth Government convened a Federal-State ministerial meeting to specifically discuss Civil Defence. This meeting agreed to the following division of responsibilities between States:

Commonwealth Government

1. Provide the States with information on the strategic situation and on possible forms and scales of attack, and give national guidance on Civil Defence policy;
2. Organise Civil Defence in Commonwealth Territories;
3. Arrange such cooperation between Commonwealth and State as is necessary to ensure the effectiveness of the Civil Defence planning and preparations and provide assistance in the implementation thereof as agreed with the States;

4. Provide advanced training facilities for selected students in consultation with the States;
5. Provide, in consultation with the States, manuals and other documents for Civil Defence training and the information of the public;
6. Supply to the States scientific and technical information on Civil Defence matters;
7. Arrange for cooperation by Commonwealth Government Departments and Authorities and the Armed Forces with State Civil Defence organisations;
8. Arrange for interstate and Commonwealth assistance as necessary in an emergency; and
9. Prepare Commonwealth Civil Defence legislation as may be required.

State Governments

1. Establish and operate a State Civil Defence organisation including voluntary Civil Defence services;
2. Coordinate State and Local Government services and other services in Civil Defence activities;
3. Civil defence planning and preparations in conjunction with the Commonwealth and other States;
4. Prepare legislation required for Civil Defence;
5. The publication and dissemination of information, advice and instructions on Civil Defence;
6. Supply to the Commonwealth scientific and technical information on Civil Defence matters resulting from investigations by State Department and Authorities; and
7. Liaise and cooperate with neighbouring States or Commonwealth Territories on all Civil Defence matters of common interest.

Following the 1966 meeting there was no apparent change in the level or direction of Commonwealth Civil Defence activities until the creation of the Natural Disasters Organisation (NDO) in 1974.

The NDO was deemed to have included the responsibilities of the Commonwealth, however this was not made explicit in the documentation put to the Government.

After 1966, the post-war Civil Defence directorates in the States were remodelled into State Emergency Services.

Civil Defence Warden signs were attached to many residences

(photo G Hall)

1974

In early 1974, a series of major floods in Queensland and northern New South Wales highlighted organisational problems associated with disaster relief.

With no apparent change in the level or direction of Commonwealth Civil Defence activities since the 1966 meeting, a new organisation was created as a Commonwealth body.

The Natural Disasters Organisation (NDO) commenced operation on 2 July 1974. While the NDO was deemed to have included the responsibilities of the Commonwealth Government, it was not made explicit in the documentation put to the Government.

Functions

The NDO was responsible for the co-ordination of all Civil Defence and emergency relief operations together with the co-ordinated use of National resources through its National Emergency Operations Centre.

Role

The NDO specifically directed federal programmes of equipment and finance for Civil Defence and emergency services:

1. Co-ordinated research, prepared plans for coping with natural disasters, and directed information dissemination.
2. Via the Civil Defence School at Mt. Macedon Victoria, it provided a National training function for State Civil Defence organisations.

At that time the Natural Disasters Organisation appeared to have no legislative authority. On 2 July 1974, Executive Council Minute No.155 announced the appointment of Major-General Sir Alan Stretton CBE, AO as the Natural Disasters Organisation's first Director-General.

The Natural Disasters Organisation was deemed to have included the responsibilities of the Commonwealth. However, this was not made explicit in the documentation put to the Government.

1993

The Natural Disasters Organisation was renamed Emergency Management Australia (EMA). While emergency management in Australia remained a State-based activity, the Commonwealth undertook a variety of support roles, particularly in financial assistance to States.

EMA was the Commonwealth agency through which the Attorney General exercised responsibility for Australia's emergency management matters.

EMA's prime functions were, in the event of a disaster or emergency, to coordinate Commonwealth physical assistance to States and Territories and assist them to develop their emergency management capabilities. The EMA had an additional function of assisting in the development, coordination and support of effective National emergency management arrangements.

2002

The Commonwealth Counter Disaster Task Force (CCDTF) was the peak Commonwealth body with emergency management responsibilities.

The CCDTF was comprised of representatives of Commonwealth Government departments and agencies. This interdepartmental committee was responsible to the Minister for Defence and provided policy advice on emergency response matters. It was chaired by the Department of Prime Minister and Cabinet.

The Australian Emergency Management Committee (AEMC) was Australia's peak consultative emergency management forum.

AEMC, chaired by the Director General, Emergency Management Australia, comprised chairpersons and executive officers of State emergency management committees.

The AEMC met annually to provide advice and direction on the coordination and advancement of Commonwealth and State/Territory interests in emergency management procedures and arrangements.

2015

The Australian Emergency Management Institute at Mount Macedon, was an emergency management training campus, providing training to emergency managers from across Australia, including the SES, Police, Red Cross, fire agencies, Salvation Army and Local Government officers for over fifty years. Many Staff and Volunteers from WA received their core training at short residential courses at this Institute.

Previous names for this college were Australian Counter Disaster College (ACDC), the National Emergency Services College (NESC) and the Civil Defence School.

In 2015 the federal government transitioned the Australian Emergency Management Institute into a Canberra-based virtual institute as a finance saving exercise.

The Mt Macedon short residential courses were then outsourced or replaced in 2015/16 by an online service from Canberra.

The Mt Macedon Institute had forty-four employees who were relocated or left employment.

The institute played an active role in implementing the findings of the royal commission into the Black Saturday bushfires.

The State Emergency Service and Civil Defence as a Role

The following paper was compiled in 2004 by State Emergency Service District Manager Colin Brown.

The Civil Defence Role

Overview

Civil Defence is broadly defined as protection of the civil population from effects of armed conflict.

The State Emergency Service, which the WA Department of Fire and Emergency Services has a general responsibility for, under the FES act (1998), has as its origins a Civil Defence background.

In 1956, the organisation that we know as the State Emergency Service, was called the WA Civil Defence Organisation. By 1961 this became the Civil Defence and Emergency Service of WA.

Between 1977 and 1981 the organisation changed its name to WA Volunteer Emergency Service (WA VES) and then to WA State Emergency Service (WASES).

Throughout this period, ties were maintained with the role of Civil Defence. On January 1, 1999, the WA State Emergency Service became a Division of the new Fire and Emergency Services Authority (FESA).

Geneva Convention and the 1977 Additional Protocol

Australia has ratified (circa 1991) the 1977 "Protocols Additional" to the Geneva Convention Protocols of 1949.

Protocol 1 (Article 61) gives the following definition of Civil Defence as well as listing 15 specific humanitarian roles that apply to Australia under International Law.

Civil Defence means the performance of some or all of the under mentioned humanitarian tasks intended to protect the civilian population against the dangers, and to help it to recover from the immediate effects, of hostilities or disasters and also to provide the conditions necessary for its survival.

The 15 humanitarian tasks are:

1. Warning
2. Evacuation
3. Management of shelters
4. Management of blackout measures
5. Rescue
6. Medical services, including first aid, and religious assistance
7. Firefighting
8. Detection and marking of danger areas
9. Decontamination and similar protective measures
10. Provision of emergency accommodation and supplies
11. Emergency assistance in the restoration and maintenance of order in distressed areas
12. Emergency repair of indispensable public utilities
13. Emergency disposal of the dead
14. Assistance in the prevention of objects essential for survival
15. Complementary activities necessary to carry out any of the tasks mentioned above, including, but not limited to, planning and organisation.

As a result of this definition the functions of Civil Defence can be summarized as:

1. protecting the civil population against the effects of hostilities or disasters
2. assisting the civil population in recovering from the immediate effects of hostilities or disasters: and
3. providing the conditions necessary for the survival of the civil population.

Who May Be Designated Civil Defence:

All agencies with responsibilities for carrying out any of the 15 listed humanitarian tasks and which have not been assigned to support the military Defence effort are entitled to be designated as Civil Defence by competent authorities at Commonwealth or State level. Eligible agencies include WA Police Service, fire, ambulance, State Emergency Service, public utilities, emergency planning committees, providers of welfare services and any other organisation rendering humanitarian assistance.

Role in Civil Defence

Clearly from the 15 humanitarian tasks listed in Article 61 of Protocol 1, Additional to the Geneva Convention, the state authority with the responsibility for the fire and emergency services in WA, would have an important role to play in Civil Defence. This would be achieved by an extension to our peacetime roles and responsibilities and would not require any additional training or the provision of any specialist equipment should that state government department be required to discharge its Civil Defence responsibilities during time of hostilities.

What Would Be Required

To access "Civil Defence Protection from Enemy Action" all participants must display the Civil Defence symbol (blue triangle on orange background) on:

1. Personnel
2. Equipment
3. Facilities

and carry a Civil Defence Identification Card

(The identification cards issued in the 1980s to State Emergency Service volunteers were a laminated card with photo ID that displayed the Civil Defence Symbol).

The question then being debated by the Commonwealth Civil Defence Committee was:

"Do we supply those organizations, who would have responsibility for the humanitarian tasks listed in Protocol 1, with I.D cards, equipment and facilities, and marking such things as tabards, magnetic vehicle markings etc. now, or do we assume that in any deterioration of international relations that might result in a threat to Australia's sovereignty, will have enough lead-time for the production and issue of I.D Cards and display material."

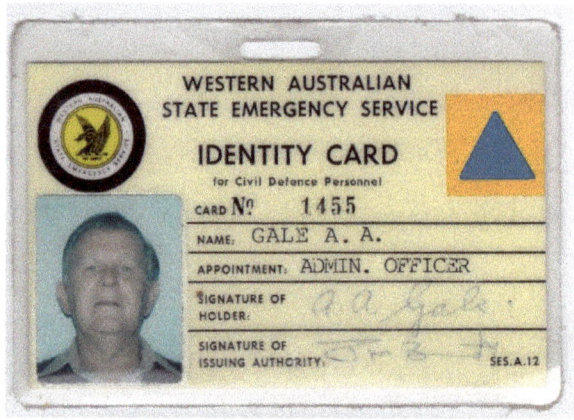

Copy of WA SES ID Card with international symbol for Civil Defence – circa 1980s

(courtesy A Gale)

Post War Civil Defence Equipment

In the post war years there were a lot of Civil Defence booklets and equipment located in many country towns. These were in readiness for any hostilities that may arise.

These items were generally located in the wheatbelt and as far north as Exmouth.

Many SES Units inherited this equipment as they transitioned from Civil Defence to SES.

This equipment included items such as:

- welfare kits consisting of a teapot and 12 cups,
- gas masks
- dosimeters (for exposure to ionizing radiation)
- cardboard wheels to calculate exposure to radiation

- bundles of manila rope – various sizes
- extension ladders – wooden (short and long)
- long lengths of steel wire rope (SWR)
- short wire bonds (SWR)
- chains and shackles – various sizes
- hand augers
- cold chisels
- multipurpose saws
- gympie hammers
- sledgehammers
- shovels, rakes and picks
- crow bars
- heavy steel pickets
- heavy steel pulley blocks
- hand operated water pump
- canvas stretchers
- canvas webbing bands
- canvas manpacks
- World War II first aid kits

The Civil Defence booklets were found at several locations around the state and all were printed or reprinted from "His/Her Majesty's Stationary Office".

The following are photos of some of the booklets:

HOME OFFICE
CIVIL DEFENCE

Manual of Basic Training

VOLUME II

BASIC CHEMICAL WARFARE

PAMPHLET No. 1

LONDON: HIS MAJESTY'S STATIONERY OFFICE
1949

ONE SHILLING NET

HOME OFFICE
CIVIL DEFENCE

RESTRICTED

The information given in this document is not to be communicated either directly or indirectly, to the Press or to any person not authorised to receive it.

Manual for Technical Reconnaissance Officers
PART 2

THE DETECTION AND IDENTIFICATION OF WAR GASES

LONDON : HER MAJESTY'S STATIONERY OFFICE : 1953

Copies will be sold only on written application to H.M. Stationery Office, P.O. Box 569, London, S.E.1, by:—A Clerk to a Local Authority, A Chief Constable, A Chief Officer of a Fire Brigade, The Principal of a Public Utility Company or Industrial or Commercial concern or Institution, County Secretaries of the St. John Ambulance Brigade, British Red Cross Society, St. Andrew's Ambulance Association, Headquarters Women's Voluntary Services.

PRICE TWO SHILLINGS NET

Detection and Identification of war Gases

HOME OFFICE
CIVIL DEFENCE

Manual of Basic Training
VOLUME II

BIOLOGICAL
WARFARE

PAMPHLET No. 7
(PROVISIONAL)
(Reprinted 1955 including Amendments No. 1)

LONDON: HER MAJESTY'S STATIONERY OFFICE
1955
Price 1s. 6d. NET

Air Raid Precautions

MEMORANDUM No. 7

(1st Edition)

PERSONNEL REQUIREMENTS FOR AIR RAID GENERAL AND FIRE PRECAUTIONS SERVICES, AND THE POLICE SERVICE

Issued by the Home Office and the Scottish Office

(Reprinted with the permission of the Controller, His Majesty's Stationery Office, London.)

By Authority: L. F. JOHNSTON, C'wealth Govt. Printer, Canberra.

Air Raid Precautions

AIR RAID PRECAUTIONS
MEMORANDUM No. 5
(2nd Edition)

ANTI-GAS TRAINING

Issued by the Home Office
(Air Raid Precautions Department)

(Reprinted with the permission of the Controller, His Majesty's Stationery Office, London.)

By Authority: L. F. JOHNSTON, C'wealth Govt. Printer, Canberra.

Anti-Gas Training

Chapter 3 - The WA SES – 1959 to 1999

As the cold war threat to Australia abated, the Civil Defence role of the State Emergency Service disappeared, however State Emergency Service Volunteers remained as busy as ever with a wide range of emergencies for which they can be called upon.

Planning for The Establishment of the SES

Early efforts were devoted to planning, the formation of committees to examine specific aspects and the appointment of liaison officers.

- In November 1956, Mr W.S. Lonnie was seconded to the Premier's Department as the Deputy Director of Civil Defence.
- In October 1958, a Western Australian Government inter-departmental committee was established to prepare an appreciation on Civil Defence and make proposals for future policy and programming.

1959

In July 1959 the State Emergency Service was established in Western Australia for the purpose of:

> *"coping with civil disasters, including fires, floods, cyclones, railway accidents, crashed aircraft, explosions and the search for lost persons".*

The Commissioner of Police was responsible for the operation of the State Emergency Service.

1961

In October 1961, following a royal commission on bush fires, a government review into ways to combat cyclones and floods was conducted by a committee consisting of the Under-Secretary Premier's Department, the Commissioner of Police, and the Deputy Director of Civil Defence.

As a result of this review the State Emergency Service and Civil Defence were combined to form the Civil Defence and Emergency Service of Western Australia (CDESWA).

The committee also recommended, along with other matters, that further investigation be made into the necessity for legislative authority to ensure adequate control measures during emergencies.

The combined organisation functioned, by authority of a cabinet minute, as a section of the Western Australian Premier's Department.

1962

In February 1962 Mr W.S. Lonnie was appointed as the first Director of the Civil Defence and Emergency Service of Western Australia.

The formation of the Civil Defence organisation at local level was intensified and a State-wide public information programme was developed.

The following are the cover and first three pages of the Local Voluntary Emergency Services directory as at 1 January 1964. The roundel on the cover was later modified and became the WA SES Logo.

Local Voluntary Emergency Services as at 1 January 1964

WESTERN AUSTRALIAN CIVIL DEFENCE AND EMERGENCY SERVICES

ADMINISTRATIVE MEMORANDUM No. 1
1st JANUARY, 1964

ADDRESSES AND TELEPHONE NUMBERS

This list shows:

(1) Address, telephone numbers and telegraphic address of State H.Q. together with name, private address and telephone number of each H.Q. officer.

(2) The name, address and telephone number of each Controller, Deputy Controller and Administrative Officer.

Where an organisation in the formative stage has not yet appointed these officers, contact should be made through the Shire Clerk. These organisations have been marked thus—(F), e.g., Armadale-Kelmscott (F).

Additions and amendments will be issued as required.

W. S. Lonnie

DIRECTOR

Overview of Local Voluntary Emergency Services 1964

DISTRIBUTION

Established Emergency Services
Public Service Commissioner
Under Treasurer
Under Secretaries
Commissioner of Police
Forestry Department
Main Roads Department
Harbour and Light Department
State Shipping Service
Fisheries Department
W.A. Government Railways
Commissioner of Public Health
Director of Education
State Electricity Commission
Civil Defence Transport Committee
Office of Minister for North-West
Office of Minister for Local Government
Administrator North-West
Commissioner for Native Welfare
Engineer for North-West
Fremantle Harbour Trust
Commonwealth P.S.I.
Director, Posts and Telegraphs
D.C.A.
Chief Medical Officer, Commonwealth Department of Health
Bureau of Meteorology
Commonwealth Railway Service
Navy
Army
Air
Joint Service Planning Committee
Bush Fires Board
W.A. Fire Brigades Board
Red Cross Society (W.A.)
St. John Ambulance
Farmers' Union
Local Government Association
Captain A. E. Buchanan
Civil Defence School Macedon, Vic.
A.S.I.O.
Engineer, Harbours and Rivers
Australian Iron and Steel
MMA
Civil Commissioner, Exmouth

Distribution list of Local Voluntary Emergency Services

STATE HEADQUARTERS

Address	Cecil Building, Sherwood Court, Perth.	Telephones: 23 2526 / 23 2527
Telegraphic Address	"CIVDEF," Perth.	

TRAINING CENTRE AND EQUIPMENT STORE

Address	547 Murray Street, Perth.	Telephone: 21 7101

STAFF

Director	W. S. LONNIE, 10 McCallum Avenue, Daglish.	Telephone: 8 3579
Training Officer	M. R. BROMELL, 34 Kinninmont Avenue, Nedlands.	Telephone: 86 1716
Equipment Officer	H. B. MUMMERY, 54 Rosedale Street, Floreat Park	Telephone: 87 1937

ALBANY

Controller	R. SMITHSON, Beauvista Road, Lower King.	Telephone: King River Residence 259
Deputy Controller	J. A. BARNESBY, Barnesby Motors Pty. Ltd., York Street, Albany.	Telephone: Albany Business 191, 1113 Residence 184
Administrative Officer	A. W. NEWMAN, 13 Hillman Street, Albany.	Telephone: Albany Business 30

First page of listings in Local Voluntary Emergency Services

1974

In July 1974, the Civil Defence and Emergency Service of Western Australia was transferred to the Public Works Department. The Hon. Minister for Works, Water Supplies and Housing assumed responsibility for the Department.

Part of the title, "Civil Defence" was dropped from its name and it was renamed the Western Australian State Emergency Service (WASES).

The organisational headquarters were situated at Leake Street, Belmont where the State Emergency Operations Centre was contained in an underground facility known as "the bunker".

Malcolm Russell Bromell OAM was appointed the Director, State Emergency Service, at the time the Australian jurisdictions were rolling out the State and Territory Emergency Services.

Whilst with the WA SES, Mr Bromell was the person responsible for initiating the significant upgrade to the Leake St facilities. This upgrade was the addition to the existing administration building of the northern wing, which extended from the current entry/reception area and encompassed all the rooms in the northern part of the current complex. These rooms included the planning, training, operations, lecture theatre and executive part of the complex, as well as the training tower.

A section of the original building was redeveloped to create a large conference/meeting room. This was named the ***Bromell Room*** in recognition of Mr Bromell's service as the Director and the changes that would be made to the complex and to the State Emergency Service in Western Australia.

1976

In the earlier days, the State was divided into various regions to provide coverage throughout Western Australia. Local Volunteer Emergency Service (LVES) units were located at Subiaco, Stirling and Perth, along with diverse locations like Westrail and the Swan Brewery.

From 1976 onwards, State Emergency Service Regional Coordinators were appointed to each of the regions. The first coordinators to be appointed were in the Metropolitan and the South West, in the late 1970s, followed by the Gascoyne/Murchison and Pilbara regions in the early 1980s.

The new aim of the State Emergency Service of Western Australia became:

"to provide for the co-ordination of planning, training and operations to counter the effects of disaster, both natural or war caused, in Western Australia".

In August 1976, the formation of a State Counter Disaster Committee was approved by State Cabinet.

The purpose of this committee was to provide advice to government at the time of a disaster, with its function being to:

- Advise Government on action necessary to provide relief.
- Co-ordinate the resources available to Government Departments and Instrumentalities to ensure that all steps are taken to plan for and to counter the effects of a disaster.
- Co-ordinate the provision of necessary services, materials and equipment not available from Government Departments and Instrumentalities.

On 13 December 1976, the State Counter Disaster Plan was approved by Cabinet.

This plan provided for the establishment of functional Emergency Committees and Regional and Local Counter Disaster Committees.

The acronym CD had stood for "Civil Defence" up to this time, however from here on it stood for "Counter Disaster".

1977

The responsibility for the Western Australian State Emergency Service was transferred back to the Premier's Department and responsibility remained with the Hon. Deputy Premier although the Public Works Department (PWD) remained the parent department.

1982

In September 1982, a bus carrying eighteen people from the Merredin High School Hostel were returning home from the WA Football Grand Final in Perth, when it ran off the road and hit a tree.

Nine boys and the hostel warden died in the bus crash.

All of Merredin's emergency services attended the crash, including Merredin SES volunteers. At the time it was believed to have been one of the worst traffic accidents in Western Australia.

The then Premier of Western Australia, Ray O'Connor, called for a report and as a result of this a committee was setup to assess the provision of the emergency services in the country areas.

1983

In March 1983, the responsibility for the Western Australian State Emergency Service was transferred to the Minister for Police, Emergency Services and Local Government.

A review of the emergency services in Western Australia was commenced in October 1983.

1985

In August 1985, the review of emergency services in Western Australia was finalised and the Western Australian State Emergency Service was transferred by authority of a cabinet minute:

> ***"as a separate identifiable entity within the Police Department".***

As a result of the review the WA Government approved:

- The responsibility for overall co-ordination of emergency services be assigned to the Commissioner of Police;
- The establishment of a State Counter Disaster Advisory Committee (SCDAC) for the determination of policy and the development of necessary planning to achieve an effective response to disaster or emergency situations;
- The placement of the Western Australian State Emergency Service as a separate identifiable entity within the WA Police Department;
- The retention of the Regional and Local Counter Disaster Committees; and
- The establishment of an appointment designated Executive Director, Emergency Services Co-ordination, to oversee the operation of the Western Australian State Emergency Service. This appointment to be filled by a Police Officer of Chief Superintendent rank.

In November 1985, the State Counter Disaster Advisory Committee approved the Role, Objectives and Responsibilities of the Western Australian State Emergency Service to:

- foster the State Counter Disaster and Civil Defence arrangements; and
- discharge assigned responsibilities in accordance with counter disaster plans, approved by the State Counter Disaster Advisory Committee or as directed by the Commissioner of Police.

At this time, a Chief Superintendent of Police was appointed as the Executive Director of Emergency Services Coordination to oversee the operation of the Western Australian State Emergency Service. All paid staff positions of the State Emergency Service were retained as Public Service staff of the Police Department.

1987

The Rationalisation of Rescue Roles was released by the WA Government Minister for Emergency Services. The major rescue tasks were assigned as Primary and Secondary, with WASES being allocated the following Primary rescue roles:

- Cave Rescue, Cliff Rescue, Flood Rescue and Road Accident Rescue (in locations where VFRS was not allocated the Road Accident Rescue role).

The following pages set out the new roles as decided by the then Minister for Emergency Services, Gordon Hill, MLA and endorsed by the WA Government cabinet.

WESTERN AUSTRALIA

MINISTER FOR EMERGENCY SERVICES

1 4 MAY 1987

Mr B McNamara
Regional Co-ordinator
State Emergency Service
Stuart Street
CARNARVON WA 6701

Dear Mr McNamara

re: <u>Rationalisation of Rescue Roles</u>

Further to my letter to you dated April 1st 1987, it is advised that I have now undertaken a full rationalisation of the rescue roles by various organisations throughout the State, and Cabinet has given its endorsement to the decisions taken by me in this matter.

My decisions were influenced by months of discussion with various Fire Brigade and State Emergency Service Units around the State and first-hand knowledge of the role of the units in the many rescue situations. I have been most impressed with the work undertaken by all volunteers.

In a number of country towns, the State Emergency Service groups have undertaken the road rescue role because there are no Volunteer Fire Brigades at those centres or because the particular Volunteer Fire Brigades do not wish to become involved in that function. In these circumstances, the State Emergency Service groups will continue to undertake the road rescue role.

The major rescue tasks will be assigned as follows:-

1.	Building Collapse Rescue.	—	Primary Secondary	WAFBB WASES
2.	Borehole/Well/Trench Rescue.	—	Primary Secondary	WAFBB WASES
3.	Cliff Rescue	—	Primary Secondary	WASES WAFBB SJAA
4.	Dangerous Goods Accident Rescue.	—	Primary Secondary	WAFBB WAPF

../2

7th Floor, 170 St George's Terrace, SGIO Atrium, Perth Ph:(09) 322 1833

Letter from Minister to Regional Coordinator – Rescue roles

5.	Fire - Rescue From -		Primary	WAFBB
	within gazetted fire districts.		Secondary	WAPF
	outside gazetted fire districts.	-	Primary	VBFB or CALM
			Secondary	WAPF
6.	Flood Rescue	-	Primary	WASES
			Secondary	Other existing resources as may be available.
7.	Cave Rescue	-	Primary	WASES
			Secondary	WAPF
8.	Industrial Accident Rescue	-	Primary	Industrial Rescue Teams
			Secondary	WAFBB or WASES
9.	Land Search and Rescue	-	Primary	WAPF and WASES
10.	Mine Accident Rescue			
	Large working mines (deep cut and open cut)	-	Primary	Industrial Rescue Teams
			Secondary	WAFBB
	Other mines and mine shafts	-	Primary	WAFBB
			Secondary	WASES
11.	Railway Accident	-	Primary	Westrail or ANR
			Secondary	WASES or WAFBB
12.	Road Vehicle Accident Rescue		Primary	WAFBB
			Secondary	WASES

13. Aircraft and Marine Rescue - to be further considered by the State Counter Disaster Advisory Committee.

The W.A. Police Force will continue in co-ordinating support of the various lead combat authorities in each case.

I have recently issued a press release on the matter and a copy is enclosed for your information.

../3

Page 2 of the Letter setting out Rationalisation of Rescue roles

I am well aware and appreciative of the very fine work which is being undertaken by Volunteer Fire Brigades, State Emergency Service, Bush Fires Board and other volunteer groups throughout the State over a long period to protect our communities. Since assuming my responsibility as Minister for Emergency Services I have, however, been conscious of the duplication of services which has been developing over a long period and I trust that this rationalisation will contribute to a more effective and efficient Emergency Service for the people of Western Australia.

Yours sincerely

Gordon Hill, M.L.A.
MINISTER FOR EMERGENCY SERVICES

Page 3 of the Letter setting out Rationalisation of Rescue roles

1991

In April 1991, following an internal management review of the Western Australian State Emergency Service, a number of changes were initiated, including the creation of the Emergency Management Unit within the State Emergency Service.

1992

In March 1992, an internal review of the Police Department resulted in further changes to the WASES structure.

This included the separation of the Emergency Management Unit from within the WASES. The Police Emergency Services Unit (PSEU) was formed and placed within the Police Department's Operations Support portfolio.

The PESU consisted of the WASES, and the Emergency Management unit.

1995

During 1995, the State Emergency Service was established as a separate department, which remained in place until 1997.

1997

In June 1997, a taskforce was established by the Western Australian Government to look at ways of improving planning and coordination across the State's emergency services.

As a result of the Barchard Report, the State Government formed a committee to assess the emergency services in Western Australia. This committee was chaired by John Lloyd and provided regular updates to the State Emergency Service Volunteers Association.

There were strong recommendations for legislation contained in the Barchard Report, however they did not result in legislation which was subsequently noted in the Community Development and Justice Standing Committee Report to the Legislative Assembly in 2002.

1998

In January 1998, following recommendations made by the committee (chaired by John Lloyd), and as an interim arrangement whilst legislation was being prepared, the Fire and Emergency Services of Western Australia was created as a department under the Public Sector Management Act.

1999

The legislation for the formation of the Fire and Emergency Services Authority passed through the Western Australian Parliament in late 1998.

On 1 January 1999, the Fire and Emergency Services Authority (FESA) of Western Australia was formally established as a statutory government authority under the *FESA Act (1998)*, replacing the Fire Brigades Board and the Bush Fires Board. The State Emergency Service had no legislation and was operating under a Cabinet Minute of 1985.

The establishment of FESA brought together under one Board and one Chief Executive officer:

- Fire and Rescue Service
- Bush Fire Service
- State Emergency Service

In subsequent years the Volunteer Marine Rescue Service and Emergency Service Cadets were also incorporated under FESA.

Under the *FESA Act (1998),* the Board was a representative Board with the Minister responsible for Emergency Services, appointing a Volunteer from the State Emergency Service as a full member of the FESA Board.

The Fire and Emergency Services Board of Management was formed and conducted their first meeting on 4 January 1999. Barry McKinnon was the first FESA Board Chairperson.

The newly formed State Emergency Service Consultative Committee Chair was appointed by the Minister responsible for Emergency Services, as an independent person, not an SES Volunteer. The Chair was also appointed by the Minister as a FESA Board member.

Board Members Appointed from the State Emergency Service Volunteers

The first Volunteer from the State Emergency Service to receive a ministerial appointment to the FESA Board was Gordon Hall, Swan State Emergency Service Unit and Vice President of the State Emergency Service Volunteers Association.

Gordon Hall resigned later in 1999 to take up an appointment as a Director with FESA.

John Capes OAM, from the Wanneroo State Emergency Service Unit and committee member of the State Emergency Service Volunteers Association, was appointed by the Minister to replace Gordon as the Board member.

John served as a Board member from late 1999 until 2012.

FESA Board SES Consultative Committee Chairpersons

Rod Willox	1999
Vivien Lambert	2001
Sandra Gregorini	2004

FESA Board SES Representatives

Gordon Hall	1999 – July 1999
John Capes OAM	1999 – 2012

With the creation of the Department of Fire and Emergency Services in 2012, the FESA Board was abolished.

During 1999, FESA also restructured the State Emergency Service as a Division and made a few appointments. Some of the key positions at the time were:

Executive Director
    Susan Rooney
Regional Directors
    Nial Wilmot
    Keith Harraway
    Barry Jones
    Gordon Hall
    Gary Gifford

Director Operations Support
Jim Burnett

District Managers

Bernie McNamara
Russell Hayes
Allen Gale
Gordon Tiddums
Peter Cameron
Paul Igglesden
Lynda Elms
Paul Shakes
Colin Brown
Darryl Ott
Paul Carr

2005

In July 2005, FESA had a major restructure and the State Emergency Service regions in the country areas were amalgamated with the Fire Service regions into a number of multi service regions.

State Emergency Service Units now became part of the FESA structure, reporting to managers who did not necessarily have experience with the State Emergency Service. Country Regional Directors were now responsible for Fire and State Emergency Service.

The Metropolitan State Emergency Service Directorate became part of the new Operations Portfolio reporting to an Assistance Chief of Operations.

The Western Australian (WA) *Emergency Management Act 2005* (EM Act) was proclaimed in December 2005. In accordance with section 103 of the EM Act, a review of the EM Act was to be undertaken as soon as practicable after 5 years of operation.

Policy Statements

As Western Australia did not have emergency management legislation prior to the *Emergency Management Act (2005)*, the emergency management arrangements in Western Australia had operated under a series of Policy Statements setting out the operational rules for incidents and processes.

Policy Statement No. 1
Emergency Management Information Dissemination System
Policy Statement No. 2
Standard Emergency Warning Signal
Policy Statement No. 3
Local Community Emergency Management Planning Policy
Policy Statement No. 4
Emergency Management in the Perth Metropolitan Region
Policy Statement No. 5
Bushfire Evacuation Decision Policy
Policy Statement No. 6
Change of Titles Emergency Management Committees
Policy Statement No. 7
Western Australian Emergency Management Arrangements
Policy Statement No. 8
Integration of Emergency Plans for Offshore Petroleum Operations
Policy Statement No. 9
Commonwealth Physical Assistance
Policy Statement No. 10
Procedure for Activating State Support Plans
Policy Statement No. 11
Development and Promulgation of Hazard Management Agency Hazard Plans
Policy Statement No. 12
Post Operation Reports
Policy Statement No. 13
Funding for Multi-Agency Emergencies
Policy Statement No. 15
State Level Emergency Management Exercises

For more than ten years the WA State Emergency Service used Policy Statement No. 7 as the main document for the emergency management arrangements in Western Australia.

2009

In 2009, the Fire and Emergency Services Authority celebrated the 50th anniversary of one of Western Australia's greatest volunteer organisations, the State Emergency Service.

2012

In the second half of 2012 the Fire and Emergency Services act (FES act of 1998) passed through parliament and the new Department of Fire and Emergency Services commenced operation on 1 November 2012.

Through this act a Commissioner for the Department of Fire and Emergency Services was appointed.

The FESA Board was abolished as well as the SES Volunteer Consultative Committee. See Chapter 4 for the replacement of the SES VCC.

The District Managers were now termed Natural Hazard District Officers and the SES no longer had any staff exclusive to that role.

The State Emergency Service functions now became part of that new department.

Today

Today, after more than 60 years, the State Emergency Service Volunteers are the most versatile and widely used rescue and public safety organisation in Western Australia – close to 50/50 males and females from all walks of life. The State Emergency Service is part of the Department of Fire and Emergency Services, with:

- 61 State Emergency Service units operating across the state.
- 4 SES Support Units (Canine, Mounted, Communications Support Unit and SWORD Logistics).
- 16 Volunteer Fire and Emergency Service Units performing the State Emergency Service role along with their Fire role.
- More than 2000 Volunteers aged from 16 to over 80.
- District Officers (termed Natural Hazard DOs) based in the DFES regional offices.

The Department of Fire and Emergency Services (State Emergency Service Volunteers as the first responders) has the Hazard Management roles for:

- Floods
- Tsunami
- Earthquake
- Storm
- Cyclone

The Department of Fire and Emergency Services has a combat role for:
- Road Crash Rescue
- Vertical Rescue
- Land Search

The State Emergency Service Volunteers are the first responders, in some areas, for the above combat roles.

State Emergency Service Volunteers are easily recognised by their orange field dress overalls with the letters "State Emergency Service" or "SES" emblazoned on the back.

Over the years a range of vehicles have been utilised which have included, all-terrain vehicles (ATVs), all-terrain units (ATUs), Toyota personnel carriers, trucks, buses and purpose-built trailers.

The State Emergency Service also maintains a number of flood rescue boats strategically located across the state. These rescue boats have a secondary role for resupply of communities during emergency situations.

Another key role of the State Emergency Service is to raise community awareness and preparedness relating to natural disasters. A prepared community is better able to respond to and recover from a disaster. State Emergency Service Volunteers educate people to be as self-reliant as possible during emergency events caused by any of the above hazards.

During the State Emergency Service's sixty years of existence, the Volunteers have been a part of some of the state's most significant natural and human disasters. During this time there have been very many notable floods, cyclones, earthquakes and storms affecting many areas and communities.

Wear Orange Wednesday (WOW) Day

WOW Day is an important national day of appreciation and recognition for the dedicated State Emergency Service volunteers across Australia. Members of the public are encouraged to show their support for the volunteers by wearing orange, as this is the colour worn by all SES Volunteers. Why Orange? Orange is used internationally during disasters and provides high visibility of the responders.

On this day there are a number of media events and social gatherings held to show case and thank the volunteers for their service in support of their communities. This is a way of acknowledging the role of the SES Volunteers in WA, who regularly leave their family and work commitments behind as first responders in emergencies.

Iconic Perth structures, such as the Perth City Council building, Matagarup Bridge and Parliament House, are lit up in orange in recognition of the State Emergency Service Volunteers. Members of the Upper and Lower Houses of Parliament and some DFES staff also wear an orange ribbon on their suits and orange ties.

All States and Territories hold WOW Day in May during Volunteer Week. In WA it was originally held during SES Week in the second week of November however in some years it clashed with Remembrance Day.

State Emergency Service Units

Throughout the life of the State Emergency Service and its' predecessors, there have been many State Emergency Service Units representing the local communities.

In addition to these Units, there are also Volunteer Fire and Emergency Services (VFES) Units who have a dual role serving the community. The role usually includes the SES function. These VFES Units were generally formed because communities approached DFES/FESA for assistance, as they were struggling to maintain several emergency service roles within their area. By merging at least two roles together, administrative time and resourcing for the community was effectively reduced.

State Emergency Service Units existing in 2020:

Albany SES Lot 4 Sanford Rd, ALBANY
Armadale SES 53 Owen Road, KELMSCOTT
Australind SES Ditchingham Rd, AUSTRALIND
Bassendean SES 69 Scadden St BASSENDEAN
Bayswater SES 27 Clavering Road BAYSWATER
Belmont SES 314A Kew St BELMONT
Boddington SES 7 Johnstone St BODDINGTON
Bridgetown SES 9 Civic Lane BRIDGETOWN
Broome SES Orr St BROOME
Bunbury SES Clements St BUNBURY
Busselton SES 306 Queen Elisabeth St BUSSELTON
Canning-South Perth SES Fleming Ave CANNINGTON
Carnarvon SES 11 Camel Lane CARNARVON
Coastal Districts SES Horseman's Ground Eneabba Drive, ENEABBA
Cockburn SES 71 Buckley St, COCKBURN CENTRAL
Collie SES 132 Forrest St COLLIE
Denmark SES Zimmerman Street DENMARK
Derby SES Cnr Sutherland/Derby Highway DERBY
Donnybrook SES Bentley Street, DONNYBROOK
Esperance SES 21 Brazier Street ESPERANCE
Exmouth SES Payne Street EXMOUTH
Geraldton-Greenough SES 15 Spicer Close MOONYOONOOKA
Gnowangerup SES Bell Street GNOWANGERUP
Gosnells SES 16 Horley Road BECKENHAM
Harvey SES 15 Harper Street HARVEY
Kalamunda SES 42 Raymond Road KALAMUNDA
Kalbarri SES Magee Crescent KALBARRI
Kalgoorlie SES Forrest Street BOULDER
Karratha SES Balmoral Road KARRATHA
Kununurra SES 1 Coolabah Drive KUNUNURRA
Mandurah SES Education Drive GREENFIELDS
Manjimup SES Cnr Bath & Brookman Sts MANJIMUP
Margaret River SES 37 Clarke Rd MARGARET RIVER
Meekatharra SES Lot 25 Hill Street MEEKATHARRA
Melville SES Bramanti Road MURDOCH
Merredin SES 7 Benson Road MERREDIN

Moora SES Ranfurly Street MOORA
Mount Barker SES Ormond Road MOUNT BARKER
Mundaring SES 14 Wandeara Crescent MUNDARING
Murray SES 6 Phillips Road PINJARRA
Nannup SES 319 Sexton Way NANNUP
Narrogin SES off Gordon Street NARROGIN
Newman SES Lot 300 Kurra Street NEWMAN
Northam District SES Jubilee Oval NORTHAM
Northshore SES 7 Lynton Street MT HAWTHORN
Pingelly SES 18 Pasture Street PINGILLY
Port Hedland SES Airport SOUTH HEDLAND
Ravensthorpe SES Morgan Street PINGILLY
Rockingham-Kwinana SES Crocker Street ROCKINGHAM
Roebourne-Wickham-SES 2A Wickham Dve WICKHAM
Serpentine-Jarrahdale SES 6 Paterson Street MUNDIJONG
SES Canine Section SWORD, Ballantyne Road KEWDALE
SES Communications Support Unit SWORD Ballantyne Road KEWDALE
SES Mounted Section SWORD Ballantyne Road KEWDALE
SES SWORD (Logistics) Ballantyne Road KEWDALE
Shark Bay SES 99 Durlacher St DENHAM
Stirling SES 33 Carcoola Street NORTHLANDS
Swan SES Bishop Road MIDLAND
Tom Price SES 492 Coolibah Street TOM PRICE
Toodyay SES 25 Wallaby Rd MORANGUP
Two Rocks SES 1 Caraway loop TWO ROCKS
Useless Loop SES USELESS LOOP
Wagin SES 74 Scadden St WAGIN
Walpole SES 10 Chug Street WALPOLE
Wanneroo-Joondalup SES Lot 21 Winton Street JOONDALUP

Previous Civil Defence/State Emergency Service Units;

Goomalling, Katanning, Kellerberrin, Koorda, Kulin, Marble Bar, Nedlands, Norseman, Perth, Subiaco, Swan Brewery, WestRail, Williams, Wongan Hills, Waroona.

Volunteer Fire and Emergency Services Units with a State Emergency Service Role (2020) include;

Bremer Bay, Bruce Rock, Coral Bay, Eucla, Fitzroy Crossing, Halls Creek, Hyden, Jerramungup, Kondinin, Marble Bay, Morawa, Onslow, Tambellup, Trayning, Wyndham, York.

WA SES and FESA SES Staff

Listed below are many of the staff who were appointed to and played a significant role in the WA State Emergency Service or associated organisations.

Atherton Dennis	WASES Manager Planning
Barker Nick	WASES Administration Officer
Barrett Betty	WASES Support Officer
Beer Allan	WASES Assistant Director Corporate Services
Bell Irene	WASES Regional Support Officer, FESA District Manager
Benn Steve	WASES Administration & Finance Officer
Blackshaw Will	FESA District Manager
Boulte Tony	WASES Local Area Liaison Officer
Breen Mike	FESA Manager Logistics
Bromell Malcolm	Director Civil Defence & Emergency Services
Brooks Margaret	WASES Operations Officer, FESA Operations and Planning Officer
Brown Colin	FESA District Manager
Brown Naomi	FESA Executive Director SES
Burnett Jim	WASES Manager Operations, FESA Director Operations & Planning

Burns Iain	WASES Assistant Regional Manager
Butler Les	WASES Deputy Director
Cahil Jim	FESA District Manager
Cale Connie	WASES Clerk/Typist
Cameron Peter	FESA District Manager
Cappleman Sue	WASES Clerk/Typist
Carlson Tom	WASES Director (Police Chief Supt. ESC)
Carpenter Les	WASES Storeman
Carr Paul	WASES Regional Support Officer,
	FESA Chief Superintendent
Chitty Meegan	WASES Regional Clerk/Typist
Christie Kathy	WASES Regional Clerk/Typist
Cook Greg	FESA District Manager
Cowie Stuart	WASES Administration & Finance Officer
Craige Sandra	WASES Operations Officer,
(nee Murray)	FESA Operations and Planning Officer
Davies Mike	WASES Storeman
DeKleer Adrian	FESA District Manager
Down Graeme	FESA District Manager
Driffell Reg	WASES Director (Police Chief Supt. ESC)
Dyson Russell	WASES Chief Executive Officer
Eayrs Jim	WASES Manager Communications
Edwards Ivan	WASES Planning Officer
Egan Kevin	WASES Regional Coordinator
Ellis Madeleine	FESA Regional Support Officer
Elms Lynda	WASES Regional Clerk/Typist,
	FESA District Manager
Elrick Nick	FESA District Manager
Francescini Rosie	WASES Clerk/Typist
Gale Allen	WASES Assistant Regional Manager,
	FESA District Manager
Gifford Gary	FESA Regional Director
Glendenning Duncan	WASES Regional Coordinator
	WASES Manager Administration & Logistics

Guiffre Vince	FESA Manager Executive Services
Hall Glenn	FESA District Manager
Hall Gordon	FESA Regional Director
Hamilton Barry	WASES Regional Manager, FESA Executive Director EMS
Hamilton Bob	WASES Director (Police Chief Supt. ESC)
Hamilton Lynda	WASES Administration Assistant
Harraway Keith	WASES Regional Manager, FESA Regional Director
Hayes Chris	WASES Manager Information Technology
Hayes Russell	WASES Assistant Regional Manager, FESA Director Country Operations
Hayter Les	FESA Manager Training
Hewsen Lesley	WASES Regional Clerk/Typist
Hill Deane	WASES Director - Chief Operations Officer
Holmes Ross	WASES Regional Manager, FESA Manager Operations & Planning
Hudson Chris	FESA Operations and Training Officer
Hutchinson Ken	WASES Manager UXO, WASES Regional Coordinator
Igglesden Paul	WASES Assistant Regional Manager, FESA District Manager
Iles Helen	FESA SES Training Officer
Ives Rod	WASES Training Officer
Johnson Brian	FESA District Manager
Johnson Roy	WASES Public Info & Training Support Officer
Jones Barry	FESA Regional Director
Jupp Carolyn	WASES Regional Clerk/Typist
Kemp John	WASES Manager Stores and Logistics
Kleinman Cedric	WASES Manager Operations
Lake Rod	WASES Manager Administration & Finance
Langridge John	WASES Manager Training

Leadbetter Kevin	WASES Manager Training
Lennon Eamon	FESA Regional Director
Littlewood Sally	WASES Assistant Regional Manager
Logan Gary	FESA District Manager
Lonnie WS	Director Civil Defence (inaugural)
Loveland Kate	WASES Clerk/Typist
Major Tonya	WASES Regional Clerk/Typist, FESA Regional Support Officer
Manson Angela	WASES Administration Officer
Marshall Phillip	FESA Executive Director SES
McNamara Bernie	WASES Regional Manager, FESA District Manager
McNamara Heather (nee Galbraith**)**	FESA Education and Heritage Coordinator
Merrill Denise	WASES Administration Assistant
Mews Michelle	WASES Regional Clerk/Typist
Moir Cindy	WASES Personal Assistant to the Chief Officer
Moreth Petra	WASES Regional Clerk/Typist
Newman Jackie	WASES Regional Clerk/Typist
Newman Moya	FESA Community Liaison Officer
O'Donnell Kyron	WASES Regional Coordinator
O'Neill Kevin	WASES Storeman
Ott Daryl	FESA District Manager
Paterson Rod	WASES Training Officer, FESA Operations & Training Officer
Perry Gail	WASES Administration Officer
Pipe Grant	FESA Regional Superintendent
Piper Mike	WASES Training Officer, FESA Training & Operations Officer
Pudney Jodie	WASES Public Relations Officer
Rayner Dennis	WASES Regional Manager
Rector Ian	WASES Regional Manager
Reynolds Terry	WASES Volunteer Support Officer

Robins Chris	WASES Communications Officer
Rooney Susan	FESA Executive Director SES
Rowbottom Wally	WASES Storeman
Ryan Mark	WASES Operations Officer
Shakes Paul	FESA District Manager
Shaw Rene	WASES Regional Clerk/Typist
Sparks Ron	WASES Director (Police Chief Supt. ESC)
Sulc George	WASES Manager Operations
Summerton Steve	FESA District Manager
Tagliaferri Sue	WASES Regional Clerk/Typist
Te Robert	WASES Assistant Regional Manager, FESA District Manager
Tiddums Gordon	FESA District Manager
Tonna Tony	WASES Training Officer
Umney John	WASES Regional Manager
Undy Janet	Manager SES Training
Waddington Kevin	WASES Supply Officer, FESA Logistics Officer
Wadley Mike	FESA District Manager
Watkins Les	WASES Operations Officer, FESA Operations & Planning Officer
Weeks Jo	WASES Public Relations Officer
Wesson Maurie	FESA SES Training Officer
White Bob	WASES Operations Officer
Wilmot Nial	WASES Regional Manager, FESA Regional Director
Wright Paul	WASES Manager Communications
Yates Julian	WASES Deputy Director

FESA Board Chairpersons

Barry McKinnon	1999
Mike Barnett	2003
Alan Skinner	2009

Fire and Emergency Service CEOs

Bob Mitchell PSM	1999
Jo Harrison-Ward	2005
Wayne Gregson APM	2011

Department of Fire and Emergency Service Commissioners

Wayne Gregson APM	2012
Darren Klemm AFSM	2017

Chapter 4 - Volunteer Representation

1985

The WA State Emergency Service Volunteer's Advisory Committee (VAC) was first mentioned as a consultative committee in a ministerial statement dated 15 August 1985 under "State Emergency Service Volunteers"

The statement advised *"that the role of volunteers will be enhanced by the establishment of a State Emergency Service Volunteer Advisory Committee, which will report to a Senior Officer in the State Emergency Service on Policy Development and Implementation"*.

Support from the volunteers for a committee representing the volunteers was very strong, and a letter to the Minister from these Volunteers was sent requesting that the VAC be formed.

After a year had lapsed with no action, a group of volunteers met with the Minister for Emergency Services, the Honourable Gordon Hill, MLA, to discuss their concerns. The Minister took an interest in the VAC and established a steering committee with aims, including gauging volunteer support for the VAC; deciding the structure of the committee; and seeking funds for country delegates to travel to Perth for meetings.

The steering committee met with the Minister and the State Emergency Service executive in March 1987 to discuss the timing and venue for the first VAC meeting; structure of the committee; and funding for country delegates.

Terms of Reference for the Volunteers' Advisory Committee were drawn up;

Aim

To promote, foster and protect the interests, professionalism and development of the volunteer members of the WA State Emergency Service.

Objectives

- To advise and consult with the Hon Minister for Police and Emergency Services in regard to matters that may affect the volunteer members of the WASES and to consider matters as referred from the Hon Minister to the Advisory Committee.
- To liaise and co-operate with authorities, agencies, departments, other advisory committees and organisations involved in the provision of emergency services and counter disaster planning.
- To research, implement and/or evaluate special projects, policies, resources, functions, training or other issues of importance to local State Emergency Service units throughout WA.

Powers

- The committee is an advisory body and therefore shall only act on behalf of any particular local State Emergency Service unit, the Hon Minister or any other individual or organisation when specifically, authorised.
- The Committee may exercise any function, right or privilege, provided that all such action is conducive to the pursuance of the Aim and attainment of the Objectives.
- The Committee shall act in a consultative role for the expression of opinions on any matter relating to the provision of emergency services as they affect State Emergency Service volunteers.

Structure

- The Committee shall consist of one delegate from each State Emergency Service region in WA, elected by the Local Co-ordinators in that region, provided that the delegate is a volunteer member of the State Emergency Service.
- The Committee shall elect an Executive comprising a Chairperson, Deputy Chairperson and Treasurer/Secretary for an annual period.
- The Committee shall convene a meeting at least twice per annum and at other times as requested by the Hon Minister for Police and Emergency Services.

Volunteer Advisory Committee 1987

In May 1987 the Volunteer Advisory Committee was established and the inaugural meeting held.

The inaugural meeting elected John Capes, Wanneroo State Emergency Service Unit, as the Chairperson of the Volunteer Advisory Committee, Paul Canet as Deputy Chairperson and Fred Ordynski as Secretary/Treasurer.

Attendees of the inaugural meeting included the Minister for Emergency Services, the Honourable Gordon Hill, MLA, his executive secretary, and the Director and Deputy Director of the WA State Emergency Service, Ron Sparks and Les Butler.

There was one delegate representing each of the twelve regions of the State Emergency Service.

The Volunteer Advisory Committee could now provide the 2400 State Emergency Service volunteers a direct link to the Minister and the executives of the WA State Emergency Service.

1987 Volunteer Advisory Committee Members

John Capes	Chairperson
Les Panting	Great Southern region
Steve Jeffery	Metro South region
Bill Moore	Goldfields region
Paul Shakes	Metro North region
Arnold Carter	Pilbara region
Richard Grigson	Midlands region
Peter Keillor	Southwest region
Paul Canet	Geraldton/Midwest region
Bill Mulroney	Central Southwest region
Arthur Bush-Jones	Kimberley region
Fred Ordynski	State Headquarters
Kevin Burkett	Gascoyne Murchison region

1987 SES Volunteer Advisory Committee

(Photo courtesy J Capes)

Back Row
Steve Jeffery, Bill Mulroney, Paul Shakes, Arnold Carter, Kevin Burkett
Middle Row
Bill Moore, Les Panting, Fred Ordynski, Arthur Bush-Jones, Richard Grigson
Front Row
Paul Canet, Les Butler, Ron Sparks, John Capes
Absent: Peter Keillor

State Emergency Service Volunteer Consultative/Advisory Committee Chairs

- 1987   John Capes
- 1990   Richard Grigson
- 1992   Bill Mulroney
- 1999   Rod Willox *
- 2001   Vivienne Lambert *
- 2004   Sandra Gregorini *
- 2014   Gordon Hall

* These were Ministerial appointments selected as independent Chairs – they were not SES Volunteers.

SES Consultative Committee (1999)

When the Fire and Emergency Services Authority (FESA) was established on 1 January 1999, the Volunteer Consultative Committee ceased to exist and under the *FESA Act (1998)* the State Emergency Service Consultative Committee was formed.

Each FESA service (Bushfire, State Emergency Service, Fire and Rescue and Volunteer Marine Rescue) established an individual consultative committee based on the State Emergency Service model.

With the advent of FESA, an independent (not from the consultative committee) State Emergency Service Consultative Committee Chairperson was appointed by the Minister of Emergency Services. The Chairperson was also appointed to the FESA Board as a member.

SES Volunteer Advisory Committee (2012)

Under the *Fire and Emergency Services Act (1998)* amended in 2012 the FESA Board and Volunteer Consultative Committees were abolished.

The origin of the current Volunteer Advisory Committees was identified in the Keelty Report of the Perth Hills Bushfire 2011 Review, which recommended:

"FESA's volunteers and industry groups be actively engaged through the establishment of an emergency services advisory group."

In September 2011, the WA Government Cabinet approved the roles of Volunteers who are to be recognised through appropriate advisory structures.

In November 2012, the Fire and Emergency Services Legislation Amendment Act 2012, commenced, where FESA as an Authority was restructured to become a Department (DFES) led by a Commissioner.

This Act enabled the introduction of a new system of advisory committees.

Section 25 (2) of the *Fire and Emergency Services Act 1998* states that the Minister must establish an advisory committee for each of the following services *(as per s. 25 (3)* of the Act):

- Bush Fire Brigades (under *Bush Fires Act 1954*);
- Volunteer Brigades (under the *Fire Brigades Act 1942*);

- SES Units;
- VMRS Groups; and
- FES Units.

Each Volunteer Advisory Committee (VAC), is comprised of Volunteers, DFES Staff and a Police Officer. Each service-based Volunteers Association forwards the details of suitable Volunteers, to be considered by the Minister, for appointment. The Minister appoints the Volunteers he thinks fit to appoint, but the majority of the members are to be appointed from people nominated by the relevant prescribed association *(as per s. 25 (4)* of the Act*)*.

Each VAC member is bound by a confidentiality and non-disclosure agreement. This enables them to provide high level and strategic advice to DFES on a range of matters that cannot be disclosed until any embargo or confidentiality is released.

The VACs are responsible for advising the FES Commissioner upon, and making recommendations in relation to, anything that may impact on the represented service, operationally, administratively or otherwise.

The SES VAC conducts quarterly meetings with urgent matters being considered as out of session business.

The SES Volunteers Association was appointed, under the new act, by the Minister as the Prescribed Association representing the SES Units in WA.

All members-elect are required to submit CVs to be considered by the WA Government Cabinet for approval to then be appointed by the Minister.

2013 SES Volunteer Advisory Committee Members

Gordon Hall	SESVA President
Dave Beard	SESVA Vice President
Phillip Petersen *ESM*	SES Gosnells
Mac Holt	SES Kalbarri
Mathew Thomas	SES Cockburn
Trevor Paton *ESM*	SES Karratha
Shelley Staff	SES Swan
Lloyd Bailey *AFSM*	DFES Deputy Commissioner
Brad Stringer	DFES Assistant Commissioner
Allen Gale	DFES District Officer
Nikki Young	WA Police
Helen Croke	VAC Support Officer

Deputies

Bernie McNamara *ESM*	SES Melville
David Fyfe	SES Melville
Keith Squibb	SES Karratha

The first meeting was held on 3 October 2014 for the purpose of an induction of the Volunteers and election of the Chair and Deputy Chair.

The first full meeting was held on 6 December 2014.

2014 Volunteer Advisory Committee

(photo G Hall)

Back Row   Allen Gale, Brad Stringer, Helen Croke, Shelley Staff, Matthew Thomas, Lloyd Bailey AFSM
Front Row Mac Holt, Phillip Petersen ESM (Deputy), Gordon Hall (Chair), Trevor Paton ESM, Bernie McNamara ESM
Absent   Dave Beard

An Association to Represent SES Volunteers

During the attempts to form a consultative committee for the State Emergency Service Volunteers, it was decided to form an Association with an advocacy role that would represent the State Emergency Service Volunteers on issues that were not being resolved by the State Emergency Service.

As the formation of the Consultative Committee had stalled, the WA Volunteer Emergency Service Association (WAVES) was formed in 1990 and subsequently changed its name in 1996 to the SESVA.

1996

A meeting of the members of the WA Association for Volunteer Emergency Services (WAVES) was conducted with the express purpose of revitalising the Association for the State Emergency Service Volunteers.

At this meeting, a number of objectives were decided including:

- formation of a new constitution;
- a new name to easily reflect the role of the Association;
- a marketing plan; and
- a new logo.

Later that year a new constitution was approved by the membership.

The new name "State Emergency Service Volunteers Association (SESVA)" was adopted.

A marketing plan was formulated and put into action.

A new logo designed by John Capes and Gordon Hall was adopted by the committee.

WAVES/SESVA Presidents

1989   John Capes OAM

1995   Clive Abel

1999   Phillip Petersen ESM

2009   David Price ESM

2013   Gordon Hall ESM

2019   Greg Cook

SESVA Life Members

Fred Ordynski

Clive Abell

John Capes OAM

Keith Wall

Bernard McNamara ESM

Phillip Petersen ESM

David Price ESM

Dave Beard

SESVA Presidents Award

From time to time the SESVA recognises outstanding achievements to the service and Volunteers by SES Volunteers. These are the achievements that are not normally recognised by other awards. This recognition is made through the presentation by the SESVA President of a special plaque recognising the Outstanding Achievement by that Volunteer for the betterment of the Service and the SES Volunteers.

The following SES Volunteers have been presented with this award:

2014

Bernard McNamara ESM - For forty-four years of outstanding service as an SES Volunteer and leader, SES Staff Member, SESVA Life Member and a member of many Emergency Service-related Committees.

2014

Andrae Moore - For seventeen years of outstanding service as a member and leader at the Bayswater and Tom Price SES Units.

2019

Phillip Petersen ESM - in providing an outstanding and truly altruistic service to the SES Volunteers and the community at a Unit, State and National Level (awarded posthumously).

SES Volunteers March on Parliament House

In 1992 the Western Australian Volunteers Emergency Services Association (WAVES – the forerunner of the SESVA) organised a rally for SES Volunteers to protest at the slashing of the training and equipment budget.

The protest was held on the steps of Parliament House with over 500 SES Volunteers and family Members attending. A partition consisting of more than 20,000 signatures was presented to various Members of Parliament.

President of the Association, John Capes, addressed the gathering along with the then Minister for Police and Emergency Services, the Honourable Graham Edwards MLA.

At the time this was the biggest gathering of SES Volunteers in the State.

John Capes addressing the SES Volunteers on the steps of the WA Parliament

(photo courtesy N Capes)

SES Volunteers at Parliament House

(photo courtesy N Capes)

SESVA Logo

The State Emergency Service Volunteers Association logo was designed in 1996 by John Capes and Gordon Hall as part of rebadging and updating the image of WAVES.

The logo design depicts the Volunteers and the roles undertaken:

- The eight arrows represent the five-lead combat and three combat roles that State Emergency Service volunteers were involved in.
- The outer ring is orange, representing the internationally recognised State Emergency Service (Civil Defence) colour.
- The centre circle has a rotating look to represent cyclones, a large component of volunteer work in Western Australia.
- The red in the centre of the logo represents the life blood of the Volunteer spirit and culture.
- The name of the association became an integral part of the logo saying what and who the organisation represents.

A flag for the SES was designed by the SESVA and this also formed the design for a lapel badge.

Other Jurisdiction Associations

SES Volunteer Associations were formed in the other States and Territories over the years with the last being Tasmania, who formed their Association in 2018.

The National SESVA

In the late 2000s a few SES Volunteers had discussed setting up a National advocacy body for the SES Volunteers.

At an AFAC Conference held in Perth in 2012, some SES Volunteers got together to chat about when, where and how (Peter Lalor (NSW), Gordon Hall (WA), David Price (WA), Charlie Moir (NSW), and one other).

The NSW SESVA Chair, Charlie Moir ESM, pledged support from the NSW SESVA to assist and provide some funding to make this happen.

A working group was set up consisting of SESVAs from NSW, Victoria, South Australia and Western Australia.

ACT joined the working group in December 2013 followed by Qld and the NT in late November 2014 with Tasmania joining the National Association in mid-2018.

At the working group meetings, a few ideas were tabled and discussed with the agreements on:

- Objectives of the future Company.
- Structure and voting.
- A National Council to be formed.
- NSESVA Constitution.
- Board of Directors - made up of SESVA Presidents and other Directors as required (eg Chairman, Deputy Chair).
- Councillors - made up of one-member representative from each state or territory, however it was not to be a paid staff member.

Other items such as funding, raffles, governance and preparation of documents to compare the different states and territories were discussed at these working group meetings.

In May 2015 the NSESVA was officially formed as a Company.

The inaugural Chair was Charlie Moir ESM 2015 – 2018.

Gordon Hall ESM was appointed as the Chair in 2018.

Lin Booth, WA SESVA Secretary served on the NSESVA Council from 2015 and Greg Cook, WA SESVA President, became a Director in 2019.

SESVA-BHP Billiton Buses

In early 2014 three of the SESVA Executive members, Phillip Petersen, John Capes and Gordon Hall met with BHP Billiton to discuss sponsorship of items for the SES Volunteers.

During these discussions the SESVA team outlined the role and support to the community and the other services, especially during the immediate past bushfire season.

The proposal meant that five buses would be located in the outer metropolitan area to support bushfire fighters as well as SES, one bus to be central in Perth for support from there, and two in the Pilbara.

As a result of these discussions the SESVA put a proposal to BHP Billiton for a community grant for the supply of eight buses with a 10 or 12-seater configuration.

The proposal included maintenance, registration and licensing for 5 years. The SESVA project managed the supply and deliver of the eight buses.

The buses had emergency beacons, a bull bar and livery fitted. The then FES Commissioner, Wayne Gregson APM, authorised the supply and installation of DFES radio communication equipment for all buses.

The SES Units that received an SESVA bus for their use and care were; Serpentine-Jarrahdale, Rockingham-Kwinana, Armadale, Kalamunda, Mundaring, Northshore, Karratha and Newman.

The metropolitan based buses were all delivered in December and January 2014/15 with the delivery of the Newman and Karratha buses in February of 2015.

Since then the buses have been extensively utilised in all type of emergencies, especially for bushfire support in delivery of firefighters to the various staging areas.

The SESVA buses on the South Perth foreshore – February 2015

(Photo courtesy Michelle Bavcevic)

The SES Volunteers posing with the buses – February 2015

(Photo courtesy Michelle Bavcevic)

Chapter 5 - Emergency Services Levy

Background

Prior to the Emergency Services Levy (ESL) the State Emergency Service Volunteers and Units received equipment and training considered by the government to be essential for their operational requirements, with local governments providing accommodation for equipment and vehicle/s. The standard of accommodation varied depending upon the local government and what it felt was required for that community.

State Emergency Service Volunteers would conduct fundraising throughout the year to purchase and maintain other equipment that was required to deliver a reasonable level of preparedness and safety within their community.

2002

In 2002, the Emergency Services Levy (ESL) legislation passed through Parliament.

Within FESA, the grant expenditure was broken into three areas: Fire and Rescue, Bushfire and the State Emergency Service.

The process for ESL within the State Emergency Service was multi-levelled to ensure as much input, from as many people as necessary, was obtained.

The State Emergency Service of each region commenced assessments of all recurrent costs to ascertain the approximate annual costs required to operate each State Emergency Service unit. This data, along with a membership census in March/April of 2003, was then used to determine an indicative cost to run each unit for the year.

Indicative costs to run the units per year at that time were;

- Metropolitan Units: $800 – $900 per member
- Pilbara/Kimberley Units: $1200 – $1400 per member
- Other Regional Units: $1000 – $1200 per member

A Capital Grants Committee for the State Emergency Service was formed, consisting of:

- Local Government representative
- SES volunteer representative (Rockingham-Kwinana SES Unit Manager, Mike Wadley)
- SES staff representative (Gordon Hall)
- FESA chairperson
- SES Executive Director

The Grants Committee was altered for the 2006/07 financial year with the SES Executive Director and the SES staff representative being deleted.

The State Emergency Service Process

At the inception of the ESL process it was expected that there would be a transitional period of four to five years. It would take this long for Local Governments and State Emergency Service units to determine the actual costs and to show any costs hidden elsewhere within the unit or Local Government. Much of this was a result of the survival mode of many units who relied on the goodwill of organisations and people within Local Government to assist them.

For the first four funding years, the ESL letter and manual went to Local Government late in November and submissions were to be in by the end of January. For the 2007/08 financial year the manual went out in November and submissions required by 20 December.

Some State Emergency Service unit applications for recurrent funding was artificially low as some Local Governments and units did not understand what was paid for by Local Government, especially with certain costs hidden in other areas, or what the unit was required to fund.

SES staff believed in consultation with Local Government and SES volunteers. Under the guidance of the Executive Director of the State Emergency Service, Susan Rooney, a process was developed by the SES that involved all stakeholders. This process was successfully used for the 2003/04, 2004/05 and 2005/06 financial years.

- The SES unit submitted a grant application to Local Government (Local Government Grants Scheme application).
- The Local Government forwarded a copy of the application to the SES/DFES District Manager responsible for that area.
- The District Manager checked the SES component of the application. Where it did not fit within expected costs, or had anomalies, they would then work through the matter with Local Government and the SES unit.
- The District Managers met with their Regional Director looking for anomalies or other matters that needed to be addressed. A priority list for the capital applications in the region was determined at this meeting.
- The Regional Directors met and went through each unit's recurrent budget with a representative from finance to ensure the applications fitted within the financial allocation for SES recurrent budgets. At this time, the capital priorities at a state level were determined.
- The Capital Grants Committee then met and endorsed, or otherwise, the list of capital items recommended for approval.

The Current Situation

The Local Government Grants Scheme (LGGS) is used for Local Governments to apply to DFES for operating and capital grants for the funding of the SES units (from the ESL).

In some cases, DFES has taken on the responsibility for direct funding of SES units (from the ESL).

It took some units four to five years to establish the appropriate budget levels for effective management of their SES unit. This included identifying the hidden costs and other costs that Local Government and others had been paying in the past.

Chapter 6 - Australian Awards for Outstanding Service

Medal of the Order of Australia

The Medal of the Order of Australia (OAM) was instituted by Her Majesty, The Queen, on 14 February 1975, establishing:

"an Australian society of honour for the purpose of according recognition to Australian citizens and other persons for achievement or for meritorious service"

The OAM comprises a General Division and a Military Division.

Australian citizens, including members of the Defence Force, are eligible to receive awards in the General Division.

Awards of the Medal of the Order of Australia are made for service worthy of particular recognition.

WA SES Volunteers awarded the Medal of the Order of Australia

1994 Norman Stanley **Herold**

1996 Gregory Bruce **Withnell**

1997 Neil **Davidson**

1999 Michael Howard **Wadley**

2000 John Charles **Capes**

2000 Paul Arthur **Shakes**

Public Service Medal

There is a long tradition in Commonwealth nations of recognising employees for outstanding public service.

Members of the Australian Public Service were first rewarded through the Imperial Honours system with awards similar to their British counterparts; however, this ceased in 1975 when the Medal of the Order of Australia was established.

The Public Service Medal (PSM) was established on 18 October 1989 and is awarded:

"for the purpose of according recognition to Australian citizens and other persons for achievement or for meritorious service"

In the State Emergency Service (WA), one person has been awarded the Public Service Medal:

1996 James Warren **Eayrs** (WASES Manager Communications)

Emergency Services Medal

The Emergency Services Medal (ESM) was introduced into the Australian system of honours in 1999 and may be awarded to a person:

"who has given distinguished service as a member of an emergency service"

The medal may be awarded regardless of whether the person is eligible for any other award through their service; however, this medal can only be awarded to an individual once.

WA SES Volunteers awarded the Emergency Services Medal

- **2000** Stephen Frank **Cable**
- **2001** Maurice John **Yates**
- **2001** John Francis **Coates**
- **2002** Peter Stanley **Angel**
- **2003** Darren Bruce **Entwhistle**
- **2003** Christopher Beat **Widmer**
- **2003** William Vincent **Mulroney**
- **2003** Herman William **Hofman**
- **2004** Colin Stanly **Nicholson**
- **2004** Nicholas James **Elrick**
- **2005** Wayne Henry **English**
- **2005** Christopher Michael **Stickland**
- **2005** Phillip Lawrence **Petersen**
- **2006** Kenneth Rex **Pember**
- **2006** Kevin John **Wrightson**
- **2007** Joyce Mary **White**

2008 Rodney Alan **Paterson**
2008 Paul John **Dwyer**
2009 Arthur Barry **Jones**
2009 Bernard Allan **McNamara**
2011 Graham Charles **Fixter**
2011 Connie Annette **Eikelboom**
2012 William John **Norris**
2012 Leslie Alexander **Hayter**
2013 Joseph Anthony **Taylor**
2014 Trevor Lindsay **Patton**
2015 Joseph John **McLaughlin**
2016 Rob William **Crawford**
2016 James Gregor **MacLean**
2017 Phillip Sean **Bresser**
2018 Gordon Maxwell **Hall**
2019 Kenneth Gordon **Dewhirst**
2019 Phillip John **Rance**
2020 Ronald Francis **McPherson**
2020 David Jason **Price**
2021 Allen John **Gale**

Commendation For Brave Conduct

Australian Bravery Decorations are part of the Australian Honours system and date from the establishment of that system in February 1975. The Group Bravery Citation was added in 1990.

These decorations recognise:

"acts of bravery by members of the community"

A Commendation for Brave Conduct is awarded for acts of bravery which are considered worthy of recognition, and has been awarded to one WA SES volunteer:

1996 Gordon Martin **Edwards**

Citation: Attempted rescue of a youth from the sea at Moses Rock.

Gordon was a long-standing member of the Busselton State Emergency Service Unit and an active member of the Cliff Rescue team.

Late in 1995 Gordon was involved in a rescue of a surfer whose return was overdue. The surfer had been found floundering near the rocks and in the vicinity of Moses Rock near Cowaramup.

The State Emergency Service had been activated as the surfer was near the rocks and the SES Cliff Rescue team would be able to rescue him from the cliff area.

On the team's arrival the situation was becoming very urgent and the light was fading. The team decided to send a swimmer in tethered to a rope.

Gordon was tied to static kern mantle rescue rope and he then commenced swimming to the surfer.

The rope sank putting extra stress on Gordon who continued swimming to the surfer.

Eventually the rope became caught on rocks resulting in Gordon struggling to stay above the water. The rope eventually snagged, and Gordon was suspended under water. He managed to break free and was washed to shore.

On reaching the shore Gordon was given immediate medical aid, and because of his condition admitted to hospital. Gordon recovered and was later discharged from hospital.

The rest of the team were able to successfully complete the rescue of the surfer.

National Medal: For Service

With the introduction of the Australian system of honours and awards on 14 February 1975, the National Medal replaced several long service and good conduct awards issued under the imperial system.

The Commonwealth National Medal is awarded to a person:

"in those eligible organisations which fulfil the 'primary function' of their service organisation, who has completed a period of 15 years diligent service or periods of diligent service that, in the aggregate, amount to 15 years"

In 1987 the regulations were changed to include "an Australian Emergency Service" in the list of eligible services whose members could be awarded the National Medal. It was from this date that members of the State Emergency Service were eligible for this award.

A Clasp to the National Medal may be awarded after the completion of a further period of 10 years' qualifying service or of periods of service that, in the aggregate, are not less than 10 years.

Further 10-year periods of qualifying service attract further clasps.

Chapter 7 - State Awards for Outstanding Service

The Peter Keillor Award

The Peter Keillor Award (recognised as the SES Volunteer of the Year) is awarded for volunteer excellence, achievement and enthusiasm and was first awarded in 1995.

Peter Keillor was a volunteer with the Murray State Emergency Service Unit for many years. He overcame adversity, through sheer courage, willpower, dedication and respect for his fellow men. Such efforts were despite being confined to his wheelchair following an injury received during active service in Vietnam.

Peter Keillor
(Photo Courtesy Barbara Keillor)

Past Peter Keillor Award recipients are:

1995	Michael **Hutchings** - Geraldton-Greenough SES
1996	Graeme James **Down** - Pilbara/Kimberley SES RHQ
1997	Christopher **Stickland** - Mandurah SES
1998	Gary William **Logan** - Albany SES
1999	Ronald Geoffrey **Panting** - Albany SES
2000	Christopher **Widmer** - Bunbury SES
2001	Pam **Yates** - Augusta/Margaret River SES
2002	Monika **Nicholson** - Collie SES
2003	Bernie **O'Brien** - Metro SES RHQ
2004	Siegmund **Belcsowski** - Mandurah SES
2005	Phillip **Petersen** - Gosnells SES
2006	Gordon **Williams** - Midwest SES RHQ
2007	Ray **Mahony** - Bayswater SES
2008	Graham **Fixter** - Gosnells SES
2009	Sergio **Bottacin** - Northam District SES
2010	Trevor **Patton** - Karratha SES
2011	Ean **Gruszecki** - Northshore SES
2012	Keith **Drayton** - Cockburn SES
2013	Martin **Hale** - Bayswater SES
2014	Steve **Cable** - Kalbarri SES
2015	Jane **Campbell** - Bayswater SES
2016	Keith **Squibb** - Pt Hedland SES
2017	Robbie **Palmer** - Mundaring SES
2018	Stephen **Faulkner** - Wanneroo-Joondalup SES
2019	Simon **Davidson** - Tom Price SES
2020	Tania **Millar** - Mandurah SES

Team Achievement Award

The Team Achievement Award recognises in the State Emergency Service volunteer excellence, achievement and enthusiasm.

The first Award was presented in 2002.

Past Team Achievement Awards have been presented to:

2002	The SES 2000 Road Accident Rescue Team
2003	The River Ambulance Team - Bassendean SES and Belmont SES Units
2004	Rockingham-Kwinana SES Tracker Dog team
2005	Newman SES Unit
2006	Coastal Districts (Eneabba) SES Unit
2007	Karratha SES Unit
2008	Goldfields Challenge Working Group - Kalgoorlie-Boulder SES Unit
2009	SES Communications Support Unit
2010	Mandurah SES Training Section
2011	Carnarvon SES Unit
2012	Kununurra SES Unit
2013	Bayswater SES Bike Team
2014	Karratha SES and Roebourne SES Units
2015	Manjimup SES Unit
2016	Bunbury SES Management Team
2017	Esperance SES Unit
2018	NDRC 2017 WA SES Team
2019	Peel/Harvey SES Recruitment Team
2020	Newman SES Unit

Youth Achievement Award

The Youth Achievement Award recognises volunteer excellence, achievement and enthusiasm and was first awarded in 1998.

Past Youth Achievement Award recipients are:

1998	Scott **Green** – Tom Price SES
1999	Geoffrey **Gorham** – Northam District SES
2000	Annabel **Harvey** – Albany SES
2001	Greg **Mulroney** – Pingelly SES
2002	Michael **Wilcox** – Nannup SES
2003	Stuart **Romeo** – Belmont SES
2004	Harold **Nicholson** – Collie SES
2005	Andrae Lee **Moore** – Tom Price SES
2006	Ian **McMahon** – Australind SES
2007	Samuel **Dinnison** – Rockingham-Kwinana SES
2008	Ash **Smith** – Bayswater SES
2009	Keaton **Widmer** – Bunbury SES
2010	Phillip **Hale** – Bayswater SES
2011	Andrew **Treen** – Melville SES
2012	Ben **Gardiner** – Busselton SES
2013	Melusha **Robson** – SES CSU SWORD
2014	Meggan **Millar** – Mandurah SES
2015	Kirsten **Beidatsch** – Mount Barker SES
2016	Mary-Therese **Shanks** – Mandurah SES
2017	Brayden **Dilley** – Kalamunda SES
2018	Sarah **Hamilton** – Belmont/Victoria Park SES
2019	Alex **Corinaldesi** – Cockburn SES
2020	Jeremiah **Peters** – Mount Barker SES

Judging of the Awards

Early each year the parent body (SES/FESA/DFES) calls for nominations for Awards.

In the early days, the SES Volunteer Advisory Committee considered all the nominees and selected the most suitable for the award from that group.

In recent years the Awards Judging Panel is usually chaired by a senior staff member of DFES (FESA in the past) and SESVA Executive Member, John Capes, has organised the Volunteer panel.

There are generally three finalists, who are show cased just before the announcement of the winner at the annual DFES Awards Night for Volunteers.

State Emergency Service Long Service Medal

Once an SES Volunteer completes ten years' service to the SES, then they are eligible for a Long Service Medal.

For each subsequent five years of service to the SES (up to 55 years) they are eligible to receive a clasp for their medal.

The length of service is calculated from the date of joining the State Emergency Service and can be an aggregate total if the service was not continuous.

State Emergency Service Long Service Medal

State Emergency Service Medallion

The State Emergency Service Medallion is awarded to State Emergency Service volunteer members who have completed a period of five years' service.

All active registered members of a unit, including support members, are eligible for long service medallions, medals and clasps. The length of service is calculated from the date of joining the State Emergency Service and can be an aggregate total if the service was not continuous.

State Emergency Service Medallion

In the 1990's the WA SES presented lapel pins for 5 years, 10 years, 15 years, 20 years and 25 years of service. This was usually accompanied by a Meritorious Certificate. The 20 and 25 year certificates were gold embossed.

Chapter 8 - Lives Lost During Active Service

James Regan (1964 – 2004)

James (Jim) Regan was the first member of the Western Australian State Emergency Service to lose his life while on operational duty.

To date there have be no other lives lost during active service.

Jim, who was thirty-six years of age, had been a member of the State Emergency Service since October 1999. His work as a Volunteer of the State Emergency Service became a passion of his.

During a rescue attempt in the Karijini National Park on the 2nd of April 2004 the father of two drowned.

A tourist party had been in the Hancock Gorge area of the Karijini National Park when one of the party had become injured.

Jim was part of a Cliff Rescue team of State Emergency Service volunteers dispatched from Newman and Tom Price, who worked with police officers and CALM National Park rangers to rescue the injured tourist.

Late at night on the 1st of April the male tourist was hauled to safety.

Soon after this rescue was completed, news came through that a second tourist, this time a young woman, had fallen and was injured at the bottom of Hancock Gorge.

The SES Cliff Rescue team set off that night to rescue the second injured tourist.

At 4am on Friday the 2nd of April, as they were about to attach ropes to the stretcher holding the 25-year-old tourist, they were hit by a two-metre wall of water.

Eyewitness accounts say that Jim was hit by the full force of the flash flood and he was swept away.

Response efforts included the immediate deployment of additional ground-based personnel, an expansion of the operation control team, fresh vertical rescue teams from around the state and aerial reconnaissance in the form of helicopter support.

Jim's body was recovered by Police divers from a pool at the base of the gorge late on Saturday afternoon the 3rd of April.

Brief Ministerial Statement to the Parliament of Western Australia

By the Hon Michelle Roberts, MLA, Minister for Police and Emergency Services

Incident at Karijini National Park

Mr Speaker, I would like to acknowledge a very sad event in this State's history.

Last Friday morning at 4am the unthinkable happened. One of our State Emergency Service volunteers was killed. Jim Regan was the first member of the West *[sic]* Australian SES to lose his life while on operational duty.

Jim, who was thirty-six years of age, joined the SES four and half years ago. From all accounts, his work with the SES became a passion.

On April 1 and 2 Jim was part of a team of SES volunteers from Newman and Tom Price who worked with police officers and CALM National Park rangers to rescue two British tourists in the remote Karijini National Park.

Once the injured man from the first incident was hauled to safety at about midnight the news came that a second tourist, this time a young woman, was at the bottom of a gorge after a separate fall.

In the middle of the night the team set off again.

As they were about to attach ropes to the stretcher holding the 25-year-old tourist they were hit by a two-metre wall of water. Eyewitness accounts say that Jim Regan was hit by the full force of the flash flood and he was swept away.

Response efforts included the immediate deployment of additional ground-based personnel, an expansion of the operation control team, fresh vertical rescue teams and aerial reconnaissance in the form of helicopter support.

Jim's body was recovered by Police divers from a pool at the base of the gorge late on Saturday afternoon.

On Friday morning, immediately after the incident the Fire and Emergency Services Authority (FESA) sent two senior managers to Tom Price and Newman to support Jim's family and SES colleagues and provide whatever assistance was required.

The peer support network also swung into action, with counsellors and chaplains dispatched to Newman and Geraldton, where Jim's parents live.

Today FESA's Board Chairman, Mike Barnett, Acting CEO, Bill Forbes, the President of the SES Volunteer Association, Phillip Petersen and a senior FESA volunteer manager will travel to Newman to meet with Jim's family as well as his SES unit colleagues. All of those close to him must be acutely feeling his loss at this time and our thoughts and prayers go out to them.

Mr Speaker, our State has 29,000 FESA volunteers including 2,300 SES volunteers. They provide emergency services to the community of West Australia twenty-four hours a day, seven days a week, every week of the year. These selfless individuals also put in hours of training and prevention work. They deserve our highest praise.

I extend the deepest condolences of this House to Jim's family, friends and colleagues. Words cannot express the gratitude that we feel for Jim. He will be remembered as a hero.

One Witness Account During the Rescues

2 April 2014

10 years ago, today (and all of last night) was a time I will never forget.

We went to Karajini National Park for a rescue of an English Tourist from Junction Pool. When we arrived, we discovered a 2nd casualty, completely separate from the 1st incident... We completed the 1st rescue and were preparing for the 2nd lift.... I and a few others had left the gorge as we weren't needed, leaving a ranger, a police officer, the casualty and 4 SES volunteers, Gary, Jimmy, Ian and Michael, to finish the lift.

Shortly after getting to the top and drying off I heard words I will never forget for the rest of my life...

"Emergency, Emergency, we have had guys washed away, Emergency, Emergency".

A flash flood had come down the gorge system and washed the team down the narrow gorge. I didn't know where Gary was, and I didn't believe he was ok until I saw him about 3 hours later.

Michael and Gary were anchored above the flood and saw it all unfold. The ranger, Paul kept the casualty, who was strapped in a stretcher, above water and saved her life and Ian broke his wrist.

Unfortunately, Jimmy was not so lucky.

Jim's body was recovered the following day by police divers and SES volunteers from Perth.

This is a time in my life that changed my perspective on everything. It is an event that we will NEVER forget. We can't.

All my thoughts to Jimmy's family and my Orange Family from Tom Price and Newman.

EXCERPTS FROM CORONER'S REPORT (15 October 2008)

Deputy state coroner Evelyn Vicker said that while there had been absolutely no warning of the flood which caused Mr Regan to be washed away, knocked unconscious and drown, the tourists could have done more to assess their own skills and possibly prevent the tragic circumstances unfolding.

"The death of the deceased well illustrates how a lack of appreciation of the remoteness of the Australian terrain can so quickly result in a death, which could have been avoided," Ms Vicker's report found.

"In this case, it was not the deceased who created the circumstances which resulted in his death but the unpreparedness of tourists in Karijini National Park for the realities of the activities they undertook.

"Accidents will always happen and people injured will seldom be left abandoned for poor-decision making, but the death of the deceased demonstrated how poor-risk assessment on the part of individuals may well result in the death of a person other than themselves."

After Oliver Peace, a 29-year-old travel agent from Yorkshire, had been successfully winched to safety after falling 150ft into a gorge, an emergency call came to a team including Mr Regan to go to the aid of Michelle Suri, 25, who had had also fallen at a spot called Plunge Pool.

***

Ms Vicker said that even with the help of "experienced and talented tour guides", falls during trips of this kind were inevitable and it was essential tourists were properly directed.

"An over-estimation of their own capabilities by Mr Peace and Ms Suri, and to some extent by their tour guides, led them to attempt climbs which it should have been obvious needed more qualified assistance," Ms Vicker said.

"While I accept both were on guided tours with the input of experienced and talented tour guides, the reality is, when it comes to the type of terrain involved, it is inevitable there will be falls.

"It is largely a matter of luck as to how badly injured a person may be as a result of a fall in those conditions.

"It is for these reasons it is essential people are adequately warned, directed and instructed as to what should and should not be attempted without skilled input."

***

"It is my view there is a very strong argument, for the benefit of the whole community, (for) DEC (to) look at building activity-accredited leaders into their licensing conditions for tour operators over time as the facility to accredit in certain activities progresses," Ms Vicker said.

"This, in conjunction with the power to prohibit certain activities due to the danger, and incidentally consequent damage to the environment, will enable those properly supervised to enjoy specific activities safely and also lessen the impact of activities on a fragile environment."

She ruled Mr Regan's death as misadventure.

The National Emergency Services Memorial

The National Emergency Services Memorial is located on the northern shores of Lake Burley Griffin, at the southern end of Anzac Parade in Canberra, Australia.

This memorial honours the commitment and sacrifice of fire and emergency services personnel from Australia and New Zealand who have died in the line of duty.

In 2019, James Regan, WA SES Volunteer, was added to panel 13 of the memorial wall, in honour of his commitment and sacrifice.

In October 2020, the Fire and Emergency Services Commissioner, Darren Klemm AFSM, presented the Regan family with an AFAC Memorial Medallion in commemoration of James Regan.

AFAC Memorial Medallion
(Courtesy Gary Hooker)

WA SES Volunteer (Sarah Hamilton) in front of panel 13 of the memorial wall (photo G M Hall)

Chapter 9 - The Bunker

Researched and written in April 2014 by Phillip Petersen ESM, SES Volunteer

HISTORY OF THE BUNKER

The State Emergency Service has a long history associated with the World War II Bunker located between Epson Avenue and Leake Street, Belmont.

Some research on the Internet and anecdotal information has revealed some of the history about the early purpose of the bunker.

Semi Underground Bunkers

A number of bunkers were built during World War II throughout Australia as part of the war effort.

These were built as gun placements, radar and radio sites, all part of the defence from the threat to Australia initially from the war in Europe and later the more direct threat in the Pacific from the Japanese.

6 Fighter Sector Headquarters RAAF

The 6 Fighter Sector Headquarters RAAF, later known as 106 Fighter Control Unit, was setup in the Masonic Hall in Alma Street at Mt. Lawley on 11 April 1942. The Headquarters was connected to American Radar Units using SCR radars, north and east of Perth.

Between January and March 1945, they moved into a new underground bunker in Epsom Avenue at Belmont in Perth. This complex was used by the State Emergency Service of Western Australia and today is under the control of Department of Fire and Emergency Services (DFES)

The 6 Fighter Sector Headquarters was later renamed to 106 Fighter Control Unit (106 FCU) on 7 March 1944. 106 Fighter Control Unit was disbanded at Mount Lawley, WA on 21 January 1945.

A Typical RAAF Fighter Sector Headquarters

A typical RAAF Fighter Sector Headquarters was located in a secure location where squadron movements were controlled and checked by radio-telephony and every move was recorded, usually by WAAAF's, with symbols on a large grid map.

Fighter Sector Headquarters would receive co-ordinated reports of aircraft and ship sightings from the local regional Voluntary Air Observer Corps Headquarters. These reports were then co-ordinated with other intelligence from the various Radar Units in their allotted area, and plotted before the information was also sent on to Area Combined Headquarters.

Counter measures were determined and communicated to counter any enemy actions. These directions were delivered minute by minute via radiotelephony.

The Chief Controller sat in the centre of one end of the room on a large raised rostrum. He received reports direct from the fighter pilots in the air. He ensured that the best advantage was obtained, and every tactical opportunity seized.

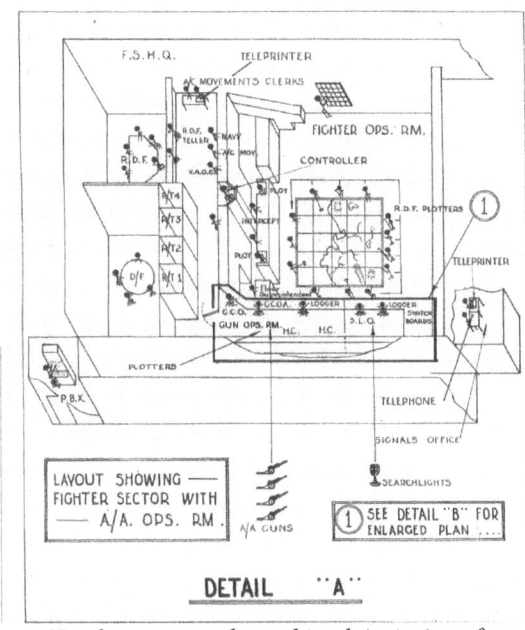

Fighter Sector Headquarters with combined Anti-aircraft and Searchlight Operations Rooms (Drawing via Russell Miller)

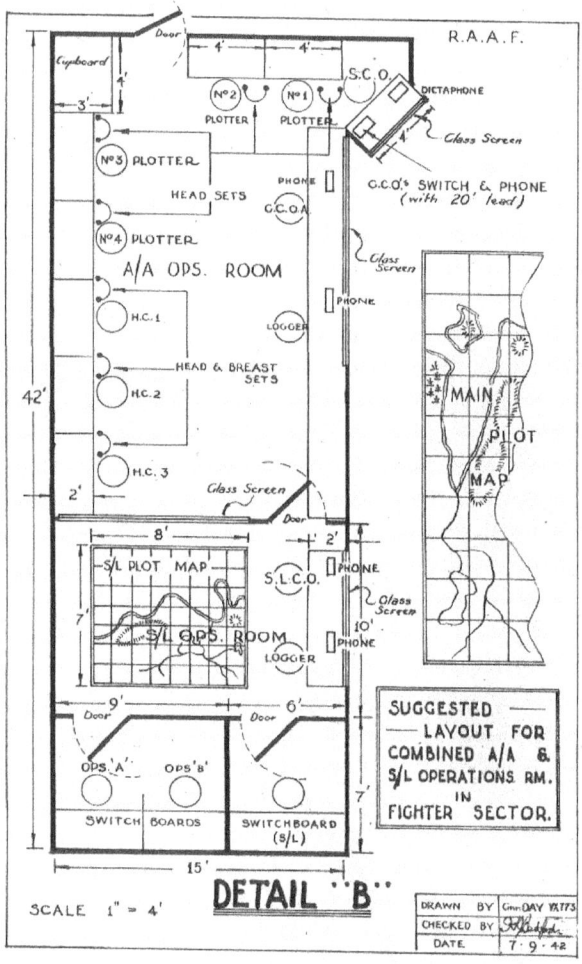

Suggested layout of combined Anti-aircraft and Searchlight Operations Rooms contained within the Fighter Sector Headquarters above

(Drawing via Russell Miller)

An Operations Room for RAF Fighter Command probably similar to our RAAF Fighter Sector HQ's

After the War

Following WWII, the bunker, was mostly derelict, it remained in the hands of the Commonwealth of Australia and was used by the defence department as part of a HF radio network known as Australian Communications Army Network (AUSTCAN). Prior to satellites, this telemetry HF radio and landline system was used for passing diplomatic and other sensitive messages around the world to Australian allied partners. The bunker provided an intermediate point for the armoured telecommunication cables between the HF radio transmitter equipment located further up Epsom Avenue Belmont, in a bush location towards Perth airport and the associated HF radio receiver equipment located at Guildford. This was then connected to the communications centre located at Swan Army Barracks in Northbridge, Perth.

The Commonwealth "ceded" the bunker to the Western Australian government. This then became the home to the West Australian Civil Defence which became what is now known as the State Emergency Service.

Dates of Interest:

- Civil Defence, Emergency Powers Act 1940.
- West Australian Civil Defence formed in 1944.
- State Emergency Service in Western Australia formed in 1959.
- Civil Defence merged with the State Emergency Service in 1961.

Anecdotal information: A past SES career officer, Mr George Sulc, explained that one of his duties as an Australian Army communications officer was to conduct tests on the radio equipment and communications cables in 1963.

In his later career as an SES training officer, he was aware that the SES HQs possessed a copy of "top secret" WWII evacuation plan for Perth. There was also a plaque in the bunker that indicated the date of when the Commonwealth "ceded" the bunker to the Western Australian government.

Use of the bunker by the WA State Emergency Service

At the time of the property transfer from the Commonwealth to the state government, there was only the Bunker and a large storage shed. The bunker was the first State Emergency Service (SES) HQs, however under the leadership of the first SES Director, Dean Hill, a complex for the administration and training of the newly formed SES was developed at 91 Leake St, Belmont. This also included an undercover parking area and a climbing tower.

The Bunker was the operational centre for controlling the response to all-natural disasters that occurred in Western Australia from the mid-1970s, until the formation of the Fire and Emergency Services Authority (FESA) in 1999. Operationally it was manned by staff and volunteers of the SES who provided Planning and Logistical support to the Operational Controller. In March 1999 the Bunker, was manned continuously whilst Cyclone Vance devastated Exmouth and Cyclone Elaine flooded Moora.

At that time Cyclone Vance was the most severe Cyclone to impact the Australian mainland and Cyclone Elaine caused the evacuation of about 1000 people from the town of Moora. All this was controlled from a facility that was state of the art at the time. During many major natural disasters, the Bunker was visited by many leading politicians including the Premier and Minister for Emergency Services. Offices were there for their use, and even a room was set aside for a Cabinet Meeting if so desired.

After the formation of FESA there was the amalgamation of a number of functions including the Fire Services and Volunteer Marine Services also based staff at this complex in the 2000s. During this period all the State Emergency Service support roles such as payroll, human services and communications were merged into FESA and relocated to 480 Hay Street,

Perth. Soon after the new Perth Fire Station was opened in 2010 the Metropolitan State Emergency Service Managers and support staff were relocated from the Belmont complex to FESA Headquarters at 480 Hay St, Perth.

Fire and Emergency Services Authority (FESA) changed to Department of Fire and Emergency Services (DFES) on 1 November 2012, as result of one of the key recommendations from the special inquiry conducted by Mick Keelty AO APM into the Perth Hills bushfires.

Future of the Bunker

Many of the defence bunkers have fallen into ruin over time. A few pieces on concrete are still around, surviving the elements and vandals such as the gun placements at Point Peron or Rottnest Island. The World War I army camp of Blackboy Hill, near Greenmount has been turned into suburban blocks and houses. There are only a few pristine examples of our past military defences that exist and are available for viewing by the public. Some of these are Radio Hill, Melville (the early HQs for Melville SES Unit), but today is a military radio communication museum and the remains of gun placements and tunnels of Buckland Hill in North Fremantle a survivor of land developers.

The bunker at Leake St/Epson Avenue, including the climbing tower, which is currently part of land managed by the Department of Fire and Emergency Services (DFES), is now listed with the National Trust.

The future of the Leake St/Epson Avenue bunker appeared to be under threat when plans for a new DFES headquarters at Cockburn were mooted. The area that was once the state Head Quarters of the State Emergency Service today accommodates a range of DFES services.

Whilst the future of the bunker was not clear, it has recently been refurbished by DFES who announced on 4 April 2014, that the bunker was to be used as a state-of-the-art emergency and exercise centre known as SIMCEN.

"The SIMCEN uses the latest audio-visual technology to simulate real life emergencies, allowing our career and volunteer personnel to gain valuable experience in incident management" said Emergency Services Minister Joe Francis MLA.

The Leake St/Epson Avenue bunker represents an important part of Australian history.

WA SES Using the Bunker as an Operations Centre

(photo courtesy DFES)

Information Sources

The following web sites can provide a very useful understanding about the history of the Epson St Bunker and large range of others that were part of Australian defence system of WWII.

- Primary Article Information Source: http://www.ozatwar.com/raaf/6fshq.htm
- WAAAF – Women's Auxiliary Australian Air Force: http://www.ozatwar.com/waaaf/waaaf.htm
- Volunteer Air Observer Corps: http://www.ozatwar.com/sigint/ach.htm
- Area Combined Headquarters (ACH): http://www.ozatwar.com/sigint/ach.htm

The author acknowledges Peter Dunn for permitting Phillip Petersen ESM to reprint images and information from his web site http://www.ozatwar.com

Editor's note: The writer of this article, Phillip Petersen ESM, was a long serving SES Volunteer who was well respected and highly regarded by his peers. Mr Petersen's distinguished service with SES was recognised when he was awarded the Emergency Services Medal in the Queen's Birthday Honours list of 2005. Phillip passed away in 2019.

Chapter 10 - Publications

WASES News

One of the challenges in a diverse, scattered volunteer organisation such as the WA State Emergency Service (known then as WASES) is how to keep members abreast of developments within the organisation and allow them to share their experiences with members in other, often distant, units. This was placed on the agenda for an upcoming Regional conference to be held at the headquarters in Belmont.

During a periodic Regional Managers' conference held at the WASES Headquarters at Belmont in the mid 1980's the subject was discussed, and various options were explored. Eventually it was decided that the most effective way would be to publish a periodic news sheet in which the State Headquarters could disseminate information to all members and to which individuals and units could contribute news on operations and other matters of interest.

The then State Training Manager, George Sulc, agreed to undertake the task to do a trial news sheet, and assess whether it would be an acceptable vehicle for information distribution. This resulted in the first edition of the publication called "WASES NEWS" being published in 1986.

Initially this was a double sided A4 sheet with the contents almost entirely provided from the State Headquarters. While this was not the intended format, the system of soliciting input from regions and units had yet to be put in place. Over a number of issues, the feedback from regional offices was that WASES NEWS was well accepted and some units had expressed a desire to provide input. It was now time to launch in the next phase of its development into a magazine rather than a simple news sheet.

George Sulc (the State Training Manager) was given the task of developing the concept and was appointed as the Editor. The challenge was to find an organisation to print and distribute the publication in a professional format without "breaking the bank".

After some searching, a printer was found who was willing to print and distribute the magazine in return for the rights to advertising revenue that might be generated. Amongst the conditions was that the publication was to be printed and distributed on a quarterly basis. This was agreed and a contract was signed between WASES and the printer.

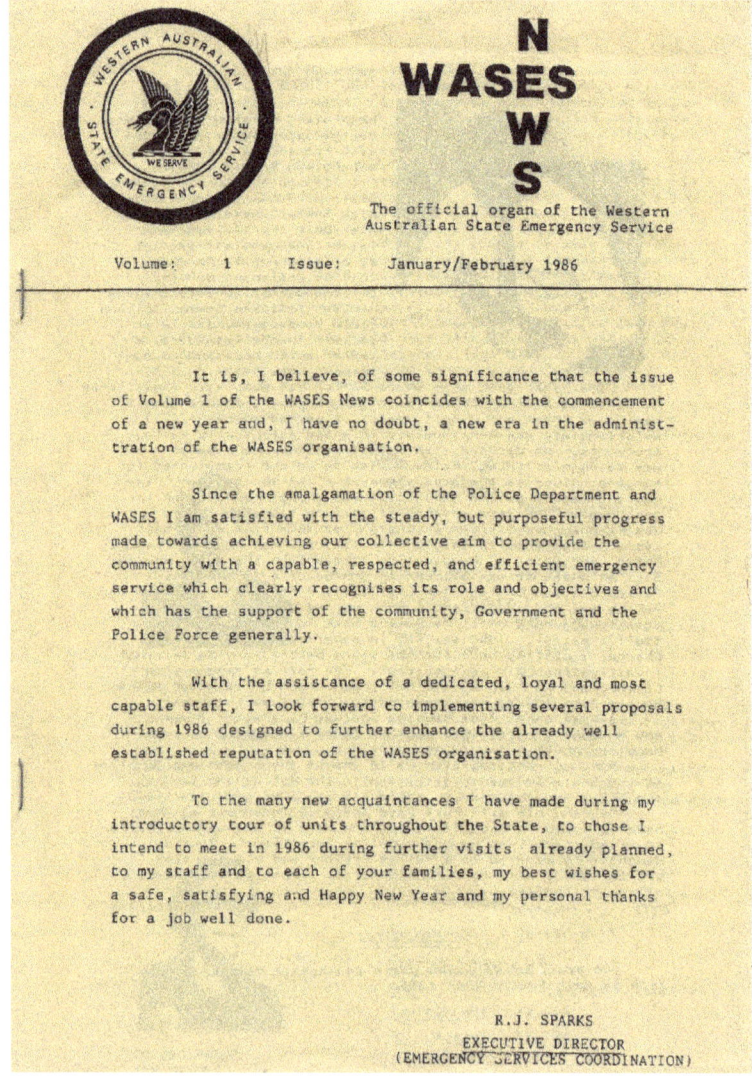

Copy of The WASES News

The Western Alert

As the WASES News was to have a new look, it was decided that a new title for the new publication was necessary. A competition was run to select a title.

Many responses were received to the competition and eventually the panel decided to adopt the suggestion "Western Alert" as the most appropriate.

Developing a format and obtaining material for its pages from regions and units was the Editors next challenge.

Regional Offices were offered the opportunity to have a section for their regional news and WASES Headquarters staff members were asked to provide articles on their area of expertise to fill its pages.

Through articles in its first issues individual units were encouraged to put together articles on operations in which they had been involved and to "showcase" their units.

As time went on many units supplied interesting and informative articles on unit activities and the publication became a valued source of information for units and individual members and a valued part of WASES life.

In October 1990 the WASES appointed Mr Roy Johnson as the organisations Public Information and Training Support Officer. The position of Editor passed to him on this appointment. The Western Alert continued as a valuable tool for the distribution of information for WASES Headquarters to SES units for a number of years, until the formation of FESA.

The Western Alert
(photo courtesy DFES)

24Seven

With the advent of the Fire and Emergency Service Authority (FESA) support functions, such as the compilation and production of the Western Alert, were moved to FESA headquarters.

Soon after this, in 2001, the Western Alert ceased to exist and a new quarterly magazine, the 24Seven, was produced covering all FESA services.

The 24Seven (photo courtesy DFES)

Chapter 11 - Training

In the Civil Defence and early State Emergency Service days the training was based around Basic Mass Rescue (BMR) of civilians in a war or Civil Defence scenario. In areas like the wheat-belt gas masks, Geiger Counters and other Civil Defence equipment was stored and utilised for training.

Civil Defence and Emergency Service of WA Volunteers went to the Civil Defence School at Mt Macedon in Victoria to get basic training and associated skills. The name of the School was changed twice in the 1970s when it was known as the National Emergency Services College (NESC) and then to the Australian Counter Disaster College (ACDC), before a final name change in the 1990s when it became the Australian Emergency Management Institute (AEMI).

Throughout the 70s, 80s and 90s many SES Volunteers and staff attended advanced live-in courses at Mount Macedon, with many volunteers returning as qualified trainers in counter disaster skills and processes.

SES Week Competitions Day

Competitions were held annually from 1976 until 1982 at College Park in Nedlands and finally at Gloucester Park in East Perth in 1983. Teams competed in driving, first aid, communications, welfare and rescue scenarios for a shield and trophies. The Swan Brewery Shield is proudly displayed in the headquarters of the 1983 Rescue Competition winning team at Northam.

The aim of the rescue competition was to test the ability and standard of training of VES/SES teams; it provided much needed inspiration for volunteers to train and innovate, particularly for those units where operational incidents were few and far between. The competitions were discontinued when it was decided to replace them with regional challenges and exercises to bring SES units together and not just on the Metropolitan area; where teams work together collaboratively similar to that of an emergency situation, rather than competing against one another.

State Training Section

The states were developing their own capability to improve access to training for all volunteers, not just those that could get time to travel interstate. The WASES Training Section was established in the 1980s headed up by Kevin Leadbetter who was assisted by Tony Tonna. The new training wing at the State Headquarters incorporated offices for the training staff and volunteers, a lecture theatre, syndicate rooms, kitchen/dining room and a tower for rescue from heights training.

SES Volunteers Bill Budney and Ray Peake are two prominent volunteer rescue instructor who were based at the WASES State Headquarters and travelled all over WA from the late 70s and through the 80s to pass on their skills and knowledge to other SES volunteers.

The WA Government Rationalisation of Rescue Roles 1987 provided much needed clarity of the SES primary and secondary rescue roles. These included cliff and cave rescue, road accident rescue and land search, among others.

Cliff rescue courses were quickly developed by WASES with the assistance of the WA Roping School (WARS) members and were being run across the state within a year. The first Road Accident Rescue Team Leaders course was conducted by WASES at the Northam Army Camp in July 1989 with qualified volunteers returning to their units to train their team in their newly acquired skills.

A Training Progression was developed for SES Volunteers which included search and rescue training as well as to the support roles for operating and maintaining radio communication systems and operations room systems as well as leadership, management and instructor training.

In the mid-1990s the State Emergency Service transitioned the Basic Mass Rescue training to General Rescue and new packages were written which included training scenarios involving modern equipment and techniques.

The General Rescue training was packaged so it could be conducted over a weekend and a number of training nights. The General Rescue training lasted until after FESA was formed and the training section was restructured and relocated to the Fire and Rescue Training Centre at Forrestfield. This was subsequently renamed the Forrestfield Training Centre.

Under the leadership of Janet Undy and later Les Hayter all SES Volunteer training was built into Competency Based Training Resource Kits (TRK's) with national competencies an outcome in most instances.

All trainers and assessors were then required to gain nationally recognised qualifications before being able to deliver or assess State Emergency Service courses.

These new training resource kits were all part of the national 'Public Safety Training Package' (PSTP) which was first endorsed for use across Australia in 2000 (PUA00). The second full revision of this Package was endorsed August 2012 (PUA12).

The future of training for the Volunteers was centred around these national training packages and were sourced from some very diverse areas (i.e. Health [HLT], Forest Products Industries [FPI] and Sport & Recreation [SRO] to name a few) and up until the beginning of 2012 the State Emergency Service retained their autonomy in delivering TRK's for the Volunteers. Soon after this the SES Training Group at the DFES Training Academy was abolished and the SES training staff disbanded.

In 2015 DFES moved away from national competencies and qualifications and has a number of new 'Skill Sets' which are varied in content. DFES believe these 'Skill Sets' make training more focused and capture the essentials of a meaningful set of competencies to perform a role. These courses are mapped in a pathway to assist the SES Volunteers in choosing the training courses they require.

National Disaster Rescue Competition (NDRC)

A team of eight SES volunteers from WA has competed in most of the National Disaster Rescue Competition (NDRC) that have been conducted in a different State or Territory since the 1990s. The NDRC was hosted by FESA in 2011 in Bunbury and is scheduled to return to WA in 2021. Although having never won the competition, WA teams have performed well and brought back many lessons to share and apply in training and operations. The focus has moved from a competition to a Challenge with greater emphasis now on learning and sharing ideas.

WA Rescue Team in action at the 2017 NDRC

(photo G Hall)

Australasian Road Rescue Challenge

The Australasian Road Rescue Organisation (ARRO) conducts an annual skills challenge to advance understanding of the science of extrication. In the challenge representatives from most agencies involved in road rescue response in Australia, New Zealand and Australasia come together to learn, exchange ideas and participate in a rescue challenge in the spirit of friendship. Road Crash Rescue Teams of five SES volunteers from numerous WA RAR/RCR units participated from the mid-90s with Challenge being hosted in WA by FESA in 2001 at the Claremont Showgrounds and again in 2004 at the Perth Convention and Exhibition Centre.

Road Crash Rescue training

(photo G Hall)

WASES Training Section Staff 1989

photo courtesy DFES

L-R: Rod **Ives** – Training Officer, George **Sulc** – Training Manager, Allen **Gale** – Training Officer, Roy **Johnson** – Public Information and Training Support Officer

Chapter 12 - Uniforms and Insignias

The State Emergency Service Volunteers are easily recognised today by their orange overalls which are the standard field dress.

These can also be two-piece in lieu of the one-piece overalls.

This was not always the case as prior to the rollout of the orange overalls the field dress was blue overalls.

Around 1980 the standard field dress uniform changed to orange.

The Northam SES Volunteers (then known as the Northam Local Volunteer Emergency Service) were still wearing blue overalls at the 1980 Competition Day at Nedlands while all the Metropolitan Volunteers were wearing orange, however for the Competition Day the following year they were in orange overalls.

Volunteer in Blue

(photo courtesy DFES)

During the 1980s the office or headquarters staff uniform was changed to dark brown trousers and a tan coloured shirt or equivalent for females. These uniforms were intended for the Coordinators, senior unit personnel or full-time staff.

In the spring of 1994 a new work dress uniform for coordinators, senior unit personnel and full-time staff was announced. The uniform consisted of khaki trousers, shirt and jumper with the equivalent for female staff. A tan skirt for females was also added soon after.

Western Alert with the new uniforms

(photo courtesy DFES)

By the summer of 1994 an appointment indicator system for Staff and Volunteers was implemented

The purpose of the indicators was to visually show a Volunteer and Staff appointments in a particular role. The appointment indicators do not relate to that person, only to the position that person occupies.

The khaki uniform for the Volunteers survived the restructuring of FESA and the subsequent changes in the 2000s.

Soon after the formation of FESA, the State Emergency Service staff uniforms changed.

All staff above District Manager level went into corporate uniform, whilst the managers changed to a FESA uniform with State Emergency Service badging.

VOLUNTEER APPOINTMENT

 Volunteer Team leader

 Volunteer Section Leader

WHQ Storeman

 Volunteer Deputy Coordinator

 Volunteer Coordinator

Training Officer

STAFF APPOINTMENT

 Assistant Regional Manager

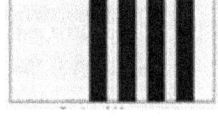 Regional Manager

WHQ Section Manager

 Executive Officer

 WASES Director

 Regional Director (FESA)

State Emergency Service Cloth Arm Patches (mid 1990s)

Epaulettes

Roundel in the state colours – Black and Gold

Cloth badge roundel in the state colours – Black and Gold

State Emergency Service Cloth Badge in shield – circa 1999

FESA State Emergency Service Cloth Badge – circa 2001

The above badge was commissioned by DFES and had the word "Volunteer" added.

Some Volunteers replace this badge with the original shield badge.

Note that the Black Swan, part of Western Australia's emblem, always faces forwards. When the badges are on both sides of the garment (such as sleeves) two badges are required so the swan always faces forward.

There have been occasions when uniforms have arrived with the swan facing forward on one sleeve and facing to the rear on the other – these were always sent back.

After a restructure within FESA and the formation of the Operations Division in 2005, all operations staff migrated to a new FESA uniform.

Operations staff were issued with hats and a dark tunic for ceremonious occasions.

The appointment indicators for Volunteers changed to orange stripes on a black background.

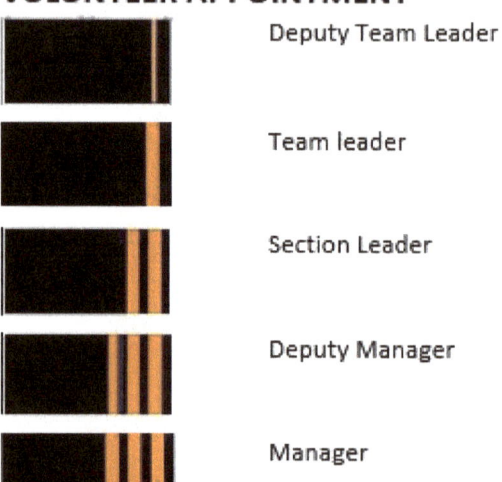

In 2020 the FESA staff changed to a dark blue uniform for day use and the SES Volunteer Dress uniform changed to Paris Blue trousers with a Marle Blue shirt.

This picture shows the new Blue uniform in 2020

Chapter 13 - Major Awards and Achievements

2007 – The Gold Swan Award

The Gold Swan Award honours a voluntary service organisation that demonstrates outstanding commitment to and concern for, the community it serves, as well as effectively improving the lives and opportunities of fellow Western Australians at a state-wide level.

In 2007 the State Emergency Service Volunteers Association of Western Australia won the coveted Gold Swan trophy.

The State Emergency Service Volunteers Association President Phillip Petersen ESM accepted the Award from His Excellency Dr Ken Michael AC, Governor of Western Australia, on behalf of all State Emergency Service Volunteers at a vice-regal ceremony in June 2007.

FESA Chief Executive Officer, Jo Harrison-Ward, was present at the event and congratulated Phillip and the State Emergency Service Volunteers Association of Western Australia on receiving the award.

Phillip Petersen ESM, SESVA President, and Jo Harrison-Ward, FESA CEO, at the Award Ceremony (photo courtesy DFES)

2004 – Awards

Tsunami Planning and Preparation in Western Australia

The occurrence of the Indian Ocean Tsunami on 26 December 2004, which had such a devastating impact on many countries bordering the Indian Ocean, raised concern among Australian emergency management authorities about the lack of information on the tsunami threat to Australia.

This made it difficult for emergency managers to determine appropriate mitigation measures.

As tsunami response is one of the State Emergency Service roles the Fire and Emergency Services Authority (FESA) of Western Australia took the initiative in forming the Tsunami Working Group for Western Australia (TWGWA).

The members of TWGWA included FESA, Geoscience Australia (GA), the Bureau of Meteorology (BoM), and Emergency Management Australia (EMA).

FESA appointed a Regional Director as the Project Director for the Tsunami Project with the brief including an active involvement in the national committees to ensure the effective planning and preparation for any further tsunami events in Western Australia.

The main players nationally were Geoff Crane, Bureau of Meteorology, Peter Whillet, Emergency Management Australia, Dr Jane Sexton and Trevor Dhu, Geoscience Australia and Gordon Hall, FESA Regional Director.

The tsunami research was conducted by Geoscience Australia which included data gathering and assessment in Western Australia.

The National and International warning systems were put in place by the Bureau of Meteorology.

The finance was provided by Emergency Management Australia.

In Western Australia a team worked on all facets of tsunami planning.

This included State Emergency Service District Managers working with coastal communities in Western Australia to assist them in their planning and preparation for an event.

Further work was done by Geoscience Australia and FESA for planning and preparation for a tsunami event that may affect the harbour and loading facilities in the Pilbara.

In 2007 FESA and Geoscience Australia were jointly awarded an Asia - Pacific Spatial Excellence Award for their work in Tsunami Modelling for Emergency Management.

FESA and Geoscience Australia were also jointly, a national winner for *"Projects of national significance or cross-jurisdictional"* for their tsunami planning and preparation in Western Australia.

Dr Jane Sexton, Dr Chris Pigram, Jo Harrison-Ward, Gordon Hall (FESA)

(photo courtesy FESA)

Asia – Pacific Spatial Excellence Award

National Award by EMA

(Attorney Generals Department)

*FESA and Geoscience Australia receiving a Tsunami Planning Award –
Parliament House Canberra (photo courtesy Attorney Generals Department)*

*John Butcher, Gordon Hall, Dr Ole Nielson,
Attorney-General Robert McClelland, Dr John Schneider, Dr David Burbidge,
Dr Jane Sexton, Dr Trevor Dhu.*

Footnote: *Geoscience Australia's scientists are behind much of the research utilised by emergency management agencies in Australia.*

The SES Awareness Scout Badge

Belmont SES Volunteer, Sarah Hamilton, won numerous awards in 2018/19 when she came up with an idea for a Scout Awareness Badge that focused on SES practices. Scouts WA took the idea up and promoted it throughout WA. The youth members of Scouts Australia who have earned this popular badge now have a greater awareness of the SES and its volunteers in WA. This popularity has also spread among the youth members in other Australian States and Territories.

Sarah's awards include the Scouts WA Chief Commissioners Award 2018, State Emergency Service Youth Award 2018, Western Australian Resilient Australia Award 2019 and the National Resilient Australia Award 2019.

The idea for the badge originated from a call out to a significant storm damage job. Sarah was a member of an SES Storm Damage Team who noticed householders at one end of the street being supported by a young girl with a table set up along with her camp oven. The girl was making cups of tea and coffee and doing her best to comfort and help her neighbours, despite the fact that her own bedroom had been completely wrecked. Sarah thought that she was wonderful, and she remembered herself as a Cub Scout, thinking that if we could teach our young people what to do in an emergency, it would be good for everyone.

Sarah developed her idea for a badge through a project as part of a Certificate 4 that she was completing for her other volunteer role as a Scout leader. Being in both organisations, it seemed like a good idea to try and see if she could get youth members of Scouts Australia to learn about SES and enjoy what she enjoyed about that organisation. When Sarah submitted her basic plan to the trainer assessor, the Chief Commissioner and Youth Program Commissioner, they all really liked it and the rest is history.

Since the commencement of the badge and the subsequent marketing in WA and other jurisdictions in Australia it has become very popular.

Sarah Hamilton during the launch of the Badge

(photo G Hall)

The Scout - SES Badge at time of launch

Chapter 14 - Education and Heritage Centre

The Department of Fire and Emergency Services (DFES) Education and Heritage Centre is in the original Perth Central Fire Station. The building was commissioned under the authority of the *Western Australian Fire Brigades Act of 1899* and was the first purpose-built fire station in Western Australia.

This building of historical diversity boasts a Federation Romanesque architectural style, it was registered on the Western Australian State Register of Heritage Places in 1989.

The building stands as a permanent and majestic reminder of Perth's rich social and architectural history. In 2011, the centre earned a High Commendation (WA Heritage Awards) for outstanding heritage interpretation of a place.

Today the centre showcases a heritage trail offering a history of each room, and a natural hazards and disasters education gallery.

Welcoming over 18,000 visitors a year the centre houses a large archive of emergency services' historic documents and photographs.

The Exhibition

The aim of the exhibition is to provoke thought and action toward safety awareness in the community by encouraging visitors of all ages to discover and explore the dangers and hazards around us.

Since the development of the Fire and Emergency Services Authority in 1999 (now DFES), has embraced all services and hazards. The Centre has evolved into an interactive educational exhibition space that promotes community preparation, prevention, response and recovery from hazards. The exhibitions have been designed in the elements of Wind, Fire, Earth and Water. Each of these elements focuses on particular hazards that can affect Western Australia.

The Displays

This display had a unique tsunami tank which was built with funding from the Commonwealth Government. The tank, when activated, demonstrated the wave actions of a typical tsunami. This display was decommissioned by DFES in 2017.

Further displays include simulated earthquake damage, fire displays and a "breaking wind" display which is centred on Tropical Cyclones.

When and Where to Visit

The Centre is located at 25 Murray St Perth and is generally open to the public between 10am – 3pm on Tuesday, Wednesday and Thursday – Check the website at;

www.dfes.wa.gov.au/schooleducation/fehc

This display depicts severe storm

(photo courtesy DFES)

This display depicts earthquake

(photo courtesy DFES)

This display depicts floods and risky behaviours

(photo courtesy DFES)

Chapter 15 - Other information and Stories

SES History

As written by Bernie McNamara ESM, past SES Volunteer and past Staff member.

Members might be wondering why a number of Units were celebrating 40th Anniversaries around 2016.

In 1976 the Government appointed a former Army Officer to lead the State Emergency Service and charged him with the responsibility to upgrade and expand the organisation. Up till then SES Units were generally run by the particular Local Government that they represented. The Controller or Manager was usually the Shire Clerk or CEO or Mayor or Shire President.

This was the Cold War era and Local Governments had been supplied with quantities of welfare Equipment to care for the expected mass evacuees after a nuclear war. This equipment consisted of such gear as furley stretchers, field coppers (ask your mother or grandmother what that was), large boilers, canvas man packs containing basic rescue equipment such as a handsaw, wrecking bar, and hammer. Shoulder bag first aid kits full of bandages (Made in India in 1946) and a dosimeter (which measured radiation). Some Units may still have some of this equipment tucked away in their store.

Some basic equipment and a rescue trailer were being supplied by State and Commonwealth authorities. Units were using donated or private vehicles to tow the trailers, and it was much later that vehicles were also supplied. Local Authorities were sending people to the Australian Counter Disaster College in Victoria to train as Rescue team leaders, Communications Officers, or Managers.

The state was divided into a number of Regions and Regional Co-ordinators were appointed to each of these regions to manage and start new SES Units in these areas. Each of these new appointees had a military service or existing public service background as the general feeling in those days was that the only people capable of managing an emergency was someone with a service background.

That is why most of the SES Units that started about that time were initially led by people that had a similar background.

As the State Emergency Service Headquarters at Belmont increased its staff in Planning, Operations and Training, this feeling prevailed, and all new appointees came from a service background. It was 1985 before a volunteer was appointed to a staff position. Since then the majority of staff positions have been filled by volunteers.

The first Regional Co-ordinators were based at Carnarvon and Port Hedland as they were considered the areas with the biggest threats of natural disasters. State of the art operational headquarters were built at each of those centres. In other areas of the State Regional Co-ordinators used existing facilities. The Metro area was divided into two regions, North and South of the Swan river.

The role of SES volunteers has also changed over the years since 1976. There was no vertical rescue, aerial observing, flood rescue, or chainsaw training. If you attended a car in a house, you cut a piece of timber to use as a prop. (Acrow Props were not issued till 1989)

A private roping school was hired in 1986 to teach SES Members vertical rescue. Three of their team joined the SES (two are still members) and we now train our own people.

A private Eastern States organisation was carrying out air searches in the east and in 1988 wished to expand to the West. They contacted the Regional Co-ordinator in Carnarvon to see if they could run a course out of Carnarvon, being fairly central along the coast. In those days we were under the Police and we were given permission to run the course as long as we had policemen on the course. Consequently, four Carnarvon SES volunteers and four policemen qualified as the first air observers. The Police air wing then took over training in the West and the Eastern States organisation eventually folded.

Flood rescue boats were issued in the early 80s to some country Units that had a flood problem, but with no formal training provided. It was 1989 before any Metropolitan Unit got a flood boat, with one in North metro (Bassendean) and one South (Belmont). When the SES got involved with Sky show they were also used as river ambulances

When SES Units started using chainsaws there was no formal training, so some Units sent their members to do the Forest Industry course (I still have my qualification certificate), It was the early 90s before we ran our own courses.

Over the years Units have come and gone. A number of wheat belt Units have folded as the population declined. In the Metro area Nedlands and Subiaco amalgamated with Perth and became Northshore. There was a Swan brewery rescue team and a Railways team based at Midland. The Midland group joined Swan SES, and the brewery team folded but some of their members are still around. One in Cockburn and one at Melville. The Mounted section were originally part of Armadale but became a Regional resource in the early 90s. The Canine section were originally based at Serpentine-Jarrahdale and over the years came under the umbrella of several Units but are now a Regional resource.

I hope that this article may be of interest to members, telling of the development of the SES over the years. I have deliberately not given names; however, I would be remiss if I did not mention Ray Peake and Bill Budney, two of the best volunteer rescue trainers who ran rescue courses all over the state in the early days.

Editor's Note: *Mr McNamara was a long serving and highly respected Volunteer and former SES Staff member. As a Volunteer, he served at Carnarvon SES, including 8 years as the Local Coordinator before being appointed as a Regional Coordinator with WASES and District Manager with FESA. After retirement he joined the Melville SES as a Volunteer and served as a committee member of the SESVA for many years. Mr McNamara's distinguished service with SES was recognised when he was awarded the Emergency Services Medal in the Australia Day Honours list of 2009. Bernie passed away in 2017.*

Other Information and Stories

Skylab

Many stories evolved out of this event but one of the more unique ones happened at a southwest unit where two Volunteers worked together on a practical joke.

One of them ran into the Operations Room shouting that he had just seen the bright lights of Skylab heading this way.

The other Volunteer then threw a handful of gravel on the roof of the Operations Room.

After things settled everyone saw the funny side.

Exmouth (TC Vance) 1999

The team, Staff of FESA and State Emergency Service Volunteers, located at the State Emergency Service building in Exmouth did a fantastic job, for the community over the three weeks following TC Vance impacting the town of Exmouth.

Many funny stories came out of this period however the funniest one involved the then FESA Logistics Manager, Craig Hynes.

The Police walked into the Operations Room at the Exmouth SES Unit and approached Craig about a matter. Craig had earlier in the day been followed by the Police as he drove down the road in the "staff" car. The Police advised Craig that he was observed driving a vehicle that was reported as stolen! Everyone had a good laugh at Craig's expense.

What had happened was, as Tropical Cyclone Vance approached Exmouth, people jumped into buses and planes to get out of the area.

Some international tourists dumped their hire cars at what they thought was the back of the Police station and left their keys in the vehicle. In fact, it was the back of the State Emergency Service building.

When someone needed a vehicle, they went outside the unit and took the most available one.

At some point the hire company reported the vehicle as stolen and it was on the Police list of stolen vehicles.

The Wrong Way Horse (circa 1998)

At 0815 hrs on the morning of the search, Sarah dropped her two children off at school, and proceeded to the agistment centre where her horse, Storm, was stabled. Within the hour she was on the trails enjoying a fabulous ride across the steep, rolling countryside, jumping all in sight and revelling in the sunshine and companionship of her mount. So, it was some time before she noticed the day had dwindled and that afternoon was upon her. Soon it would be time to collect the kids from school.

She drew rein, scanned her surroundings and decided on the track to take home. But on nudging Storm forward, the horse refused to move. He wanted to go in the opposite direction and Sarah had her hands full in keeping him to the line she had chosen. She urged him on again, gained a few hundred metres before he propped, spun, and charged back in the direction he had come. And so, the battle raged. Each time Sarah managed to gain some ground towards home, Storm would rake it back with more metres to spare. Sarah grew worried, she was slowly losing control of the horse and feared either she would get lost or Storm would throw her and be loose in the wild terrain. Already she was losing her bearings with each new plunge and bolt Storm took in the wrong direction.

Eventually she dismounted. It was growing dark and the horse had calmed somewhat in the now strange surrounds. She tied Storm to a tree to keep him contained, and as night fell, the horse, accustomed to the luxuries of a stable, laid down on a soft patch of earth.

The cold swept in, and Sarah lay down, snuggled in against Storm's neck to shield herself from the wind and share the warmth of his body.

Meanwhile by mid-afternoon, her children had not been collected from school and the school had rung home. The phone rang out. The alternative phone number was the children's father. On receiving the call, the father left his office and proceeded immediately to collect his children.

On arriving home his worry began in earnest – neither his wife nor her car was there. He delivered the children to a friend's house and continued on to the agistment centre where he found Sarah's car, but no Storm and no Sarah. He contacted the police immediately who subsequently arrived and commenced their investigations.

A short time later the SES was activated, the Swan and Wanneroo Unit volunteers told to prepare for a search. An advance SES party, consisting of a unit manager and deputy, arrived to commence setting up the search base and preparing briefings for the search teams' arrival.

Given the high level of anxiety of the children's father, caused by the hours his wife had obviously been missing, the four SES vehicles were advised to arrive with all emergency lights flashing – an impressive sight in the pitch blackness as they swept down the roadway towards the search base – and an obvious relief for the Husband that so many had attended.

The search teams were briefed, and with a local person assisting each team, the volunteers headed out to search their allocated sectors.

Within the hour, at about 2230 hrs, one team heard an answer to the "calling and listening" phase of their sweep. Focussing astutely, they called and listened again, repeating the procedure every fifty metres as they strained to determine the direction of the replies, for the valley echoes sent the sounds back from every direction.

Over thirty minutes passed, the replies sounding louder at each stop and call until, on topping a rise in the darkness, searchers spotted something sixty metres ahead of them. It was Sarah laying with her beloved Storm. Both were cold but safe.

A rescue vehicle was called in, and as they all proceeded to it, Sarah told them of her problem with the horse – that it had become disorientated and kept going the wrong way.

A rider was assigned to the horse, and Sarah helped into the back of the vehicle for an easy ride home. With a rider back on board, Storm proceeded back on his chosen course, and sprinted away to his stable, Sarah shouting after them in panic - "He's going the wrong way!"

To which someone replied: "No, he isn't."

Chapter 16 - Significant Operations or Events

1968 – Meckering Earthquake

The WA wheatbelt town of Meckering was almost completely flattened on the 14 of October 1968 when 6.8 magnitude earthquake cracked the surface at 10.59am and shook a large area for 40 seconds. The earthquake was centred just 9km south west of Meckering. Fortunately, no lives were lost with minor injuries only being reported.

By nightfall the Police and the Civil Defence and Emergency Service had a control centre operating at the showgrounds. The Civil Defence and Emergency Service response included the Mobile Column from State HQ at Belmont, the heavy rescue truck from Kellerberrin and the Controller from Northam.

Much was learnt from the response to the earthquake and the long recovery that followed. A lot of towns in the area started sending people to Mount Macedon for training ready to respond in the event of another earthquake – which occurred again 11 years later just to the north of Meckering at Cadoux on the afternoon of 9th June.

Meckering Hotel (photo courtesy DFES)

1978 – Cyclone Alby

Severe Tropical Cyclone Alby was first identified on 27 March 1978 by the Bureau of Meteorology. It was situated 800 km north-northwest of Karratha. Early on March 29, the system was classified as a tropical cyclone by the Perth Bureau of Meteorology.

TC Alby steadily and attained its peak intensity as a Category 5.

TC Alby slowed as it began turning towards the southeast. By 3 April, the storm rapidly accelerated and attained a forward speed of 50 km/h. The storm gradually weakened and passed within 100 km of Cape Leeuwin. The system-maintained winds of 120 km/h (75 mph) as it reached this point, making it one of the most intense storms to strike the region. By 5 April, the cyclone rapidly lost its identity as it became caught up in a north-westerly flow before merging with the cold front over the Great Australian Bight

The winds resulted in widespread agricultural, environmental and structural damage. Hundreds of structures sustained severe damage, mostly consisting of roofs blowing off. The most severe losses took place in Albany where most homes had partial or complete roof failure. Numerous power lines and stations failed during the storm. Large portions of the South-West were without electricity due to Cyclone Alby.

Alby's winds fanned at least 50 individual fires across the region, prompting more than 1,000 firefighters to assist in putting them out. Some of these fires turned into full-fledged wildfires, expanding at a rate of 5 to 10 km/h.

A total of 114,000 hectares of land was burned, more than 10,000 sheep, 500 cattle and horses were killed. Over 100 structures, 1,300 km of fencing and tens of thousands of hay bales were destroyed.

Along the coast, large swells produced by the storm resulted in two fatalities in Albany Harbour as well as significant coastal damage. The highest storm tide was in Busselton at 2.5 m (8.2 ft), leading to a storm surge of 1.1 m. Here, the surge penetrated roughly 200 m inland, forcing several evacuations. This led to significant coastal flooding that damaged dozens of structures. In Bunbury, water breached the sea wall, inundating homes and prompting the evacuation of 130 residents.

Tropical Cyclone Alby was responsible for seven fatalities and more than $50m damage. Due to the extensive damage, the name Alby was retired from the list of cyclone names to be used in Western Australian.

The State Emergency Service was activated and assisted many people across the lower southwest who required help. Records of the actual numbers of people involved and calls for assistance have not been found.

1979 – Skylab

Skylab was a US space station launched by NASA in 1973 and was manned by teams of astronauts as it orbited the earth. It collected vast amounts of data and images before being abandoned in space in 1974.

In the early hours of the 12th of July 1979, Skylab crashed on WA's south east coast, scattering debris across the Nullarbor and the eastern goldfields. This caused a worldwide sensation.

In 1979, NASA realised that Skylab was starting to break up and would re-enter the atmosphere. They could neither control Skylab's path nor could they predict exactly where the pieces might land.

As NASA, and the world's media tracked Skylab's progress in early July 1979, it seemed it could end up anywhere.

State Emergency Service Units along the predicted path of possible re-entry, were activated and Volunteers manned these units throughout the night in readiness for a response if the debris fell in their area.

These days, Skylab is a source of pride to the people of Esperance and the Nullarbor, who remember the lights, the sonic boom and the fuss that followed.

The US President at the time, Jimmy Carter called the Balladonia hotel to apologise for any damages and an US Ambassador and Miss America visited the Hotel Motel as a goodwill gesture.

1986 Papal Visit

In November 1986 the Pope visited Perth.

The SES had a key role in this visit by the provision of communications personnel from SES Units to man the Site Directors communications organisational networks and to adopt a state of readiness during the visit.

SES Volunteers have a key role in this operation with Wanneroo SES Volunteer John Capes being the senior Volunteer involved.

The Operations were very detailed and included all coordinating instructions and a radio net diagram.

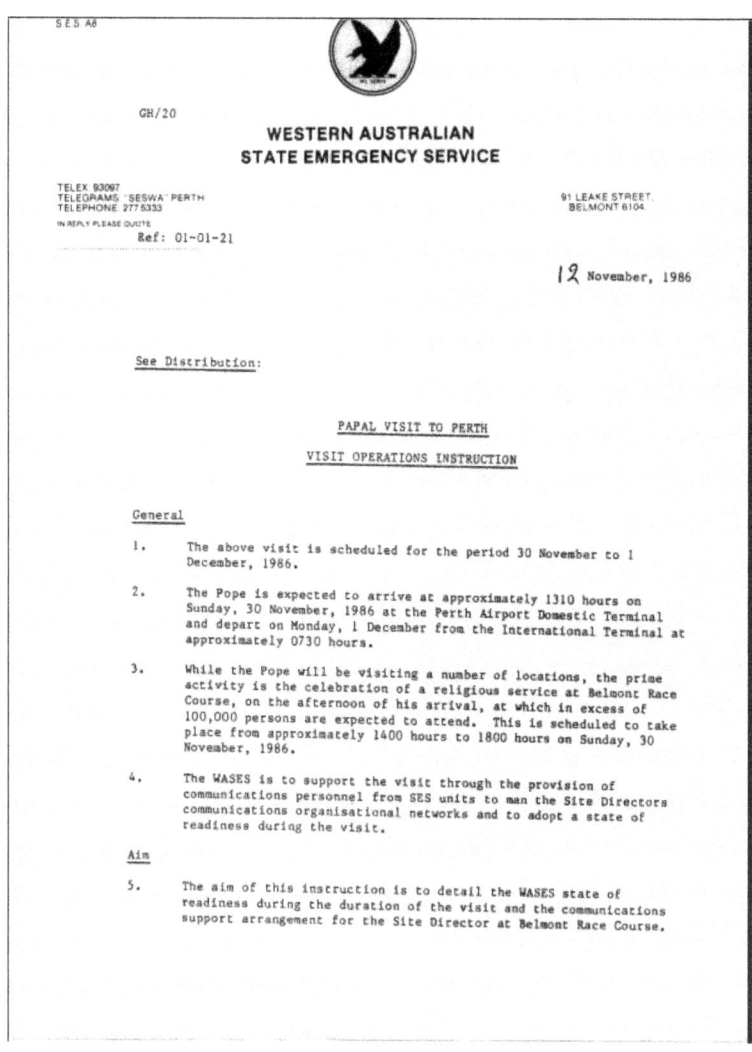

Copy of the front page of the Papal visit Operations Instructions

1988 – TC Herbie, Korean Star Rescue

Tropical Cyclone Herbie appeared out of the darkness in the early hours of Saturday 21st May 1988 whipping up high seas and gale force winds that swept an empty salt ship against the rocky base of the 100m cliffs near Cape Cuvier 120 kilometres north of Carnarvon. Rescue of the crew was not possible by tugs due to the dangerous conditions and a helicopter was not going to arrive for some hours, so when the ship appeared to be starting to break up the SES rescue team from Carnarvon was called in, along with personnel from Police, Customs, Marine and Harbours, Shipping agents and Dampier Salt.

The SES team, being led by Brain Hutton, attached a line to the stricken ship and with the aid of riggers from a tug company, rigged up a flying fox. Some of the crews luggage was removed first to test the system then the crew were transferred safely to shore after having been flung off their feet and thrown from side to side while waiting their turn the evacuate the dying ship which heaved violently in the towering seas on the jagged rocks.

Wreck of the Korean Star

(photo courtesy DFES)

The ingenuity of the SES volunteers played a critical role in the success of the operation, in particular the variable tensioning system used to prevent the Flying Fox ropes from snapping and the extreme care taken to ensure the ship's crew were not bashed against the rocks while they were being lowered from the ship into the safety of their rescuers on the shore below.

1994 – Perth Storms

On 23 May a severe storm hit Perth causing serious damage.

The damage bill is estimated to be in excess of $37m.

More than 600 homes in Perth had sustained some form of damage.

More than 250 000 homes and businesses were without power and it took nearly awake for power to be completely restored. This loss of power also affected sewerage pumping stations resulting in minor spills of raw sewage into the Swan and Canning rivers.

Two people on board a yacht was lost at sea off Jurien, north of Perth. Huge seas and above normal tides caused significant erosion to beaches, while parts of the Perth river foreshore were inundated.

Fremantle recorded 25 wind gusts of at least 129 km/h, more than three times the number recorded for any other event since the 1960s.

The State Emergency Service received over 1700 calls for assistance and the Volunteers responded to these by providing temporary repairs to rooves, cutting trees up, clearing debris and numerous other tasks to assist their communities to return to normal as soon as possible.

1997 – The Jamie Godden Search & the Gerard Ross Search

13-Year-old Jamie Godden was murdered near Byford in September 1997 after coming across a bush camp while riding his motor bike.

The WA Police activated the State Emergency Service Volunteers the following day when Jamie failed to return home the previous evening. A search base was set up at the Byford Hall with Metropolitan Units responding to the call for an urgent search fearing Jamie might be laying injured in bushland.

The bush camp was found early on day one of the search, but there was no sign of the missing boy, however Police had found evidence that lead them to the murderer and his accomplice by the end of the second day.

On the third day Police were taken to bushland where Jamie's body had been hidden. The location was well beyond the large search area where more than two hundred SES volunteers, BFS volunteers and other volunteers had been desperately searching for three days in the hope of finding Jamie alive.

Less than a month later in October 1997, Gerard Ross was abducted from the Perth suburb of Rockingham during a family holiday.

The WA Police activated the State Emergency Service Volunteers and a search base was set up at the Rockingham-Kwinana State Emergency Service unit.

Volunteers from Metropolitan Units responded, and thorough searches were conducted in bush land in the near vicinity of Rockingham's CBD.

After a week of searching the Police called off the search as there was no evidence anywhere of where he was or may have been.

Gerard's body was found 15 days later dumped in a pine plantation in Karnup. His killer has never been found.

A reward for information leading to a conviction in Gerard's murder has been offered by the WA Government. This reward was current at time of printing this book.

1998 – The Pannikin Plains Rescue

as told by Jim Ridgwell, SES Volunteer, Gosnells SES

Overview

In 1988 the State SES Cliff and Cave Rescue Team was called to respond to a rescue on the Nullarbor Plain. Jim Ridgwell was one of those rescuers and 21 years later he visited the site that posed a challenge so many years before. Below is Jim's recollection of the events of that rescue.

The Rescue

For anyone who has been in the SES for a while they will have one or sometimes several callouts which stand out as being memorable in your career. The rescue at Pannikin Plains is mine.

Back in 1989 I was a member of the state Cliff and Cave Rescue Team. We trained during the weeknights at Leake St, Belmont and on weekends at quarries. We honed our skills, read books on the subject and continually practiced. We lived and breathed abseiling. Some of us even found time to get involved with private abseiling companies to learn more, pick up different skills and use equipment which wasn't necessarily taught at SES. An example of this would be, I am still a fan of the rappel rack, must to the consternation of my colleagues. Up until then I can't recall us having doing a "real" cliff rescue before the Pannikin Plains rescue.

The Callout

On the morning of the 2nd December 1988 we received a call directing us to be at Perth airport at sunup. The information at that time was there were some people trapped in a cave. That was it! Oh, and take enough clothes for a couple of days!

The members called were to my recollection, Bob Coops (team leader) Neil McCaulay, Darren Brooks, Rod Ives, and myself. We went to Belmont and collected the gear we would need and headed off to Perth Airport. When we arrived we found that we would be flying in a Beechcraft King Air twin turbo prop aircraft which had just been negotiated into a contract some weeks earlier between the SES and the State Government to be available for just this type of emergency. It was a cool plane! The briefing finally came, and we were informed we were going to Cocklebiddy to rescue some cavers who had got stuck in a cave. We unloaded our kits and equipment onto the tarmac next to the plane and I can still clearly remember one of the two pilot's face when he saw all our gear. He started laughing but got kind of serious when we told him we needed everything. We had enough rope and hardware to start our own store. There were anchor systems made from sheet steel, steel pickets, stretchers, first aid kits and on it went. The Landcruiser was grunting just to get us there and as the pilot said, we had to cut back, or we wouldn't even get off the ground. We trimmed and trimmed until eventually the pilot gave his OK. We thought at this stage we may as well not go. Almost everything we thought we needed was in the "reject" pile.

So, we took off. On board was a cameraman from a Current Affairs program and it was his job to document the whole event. He interviewed us and had his camera on us often. Sometimes this was a little disconcerting if you were trying to have a nap and you opened your eyes to find him videoing you. We couldn't sleep though because we were all so hyped up, I think we had adrenalin oozing from our pores. As it turned out the documentary never went to air and to my knowledge none of us ever become a TV star.

Getting There

The trip over there was relatively uneventful. Just sitting back in leather seats being supplied (you couldn't call it served) coffee by one of the pilots. As if we needed coffee! The pilot told us they were clearing a section of white posts from either side of the Eyre Highway so we could land on the highway near the cave. Police were on site. So far so good but it was about now things started to go pear shaped.

We got word the highway had too much debris on it which would prevent us from landing. What do you mean debris I was thinking? OK so plan B was that we would land a bit further away at Caiguna airstrip at the back of the roadhouse. An hour or so later the pilots told us the cloud cover was very low, (we call it fog at ground level) but we would try and land anyway. The pilots seemed pretty confident. Wrong! After a couple of passes the pilots concluded the cloud cover was too low. So now what? We were getting low on fuel and couldn't land. Now I started to take more of an interest. As it turned out plan C was to divert to the small community of Forrest, a stop for the Indian-Pacific train, which was a few hundred kilometres away. We landed OK and by now we were starting to get hungry. Well, we will just duck up to the shop. Wrong again, there are no shops in Forrest but a guy working at the airstrip offered to race back home and get his wife to make sandwiches. We fuelled up and the sandwiches arrived just as we were ready to go. We had got the word the clouds were thinning out. Things were looking up again. As we flew back over Caiguna the clouds had come back in again and we were back where we had been a few hours ago. The pilots got another plan. We would fly out over the Great Australian Bight and then as we fly back to land, we would look for a break in the clouds. Seemed like a reasonable plan until I realised how the pilots planned to do it. The cliffs there are around 60 metres high and the plan was to fly out to sea and then turn and come back in below cliff height looking for a clear spot and at the last-minute lift and go under the cloud cover. Let me tell you right now I wasn't a fan of this plan, but I don't remember being asked what I thought of it either. So there we were, flying out at sea at somewhere about 40 metres above the sea and looking out the front window and all I could see was cliffs. Just as planned at the last moment the pilots lifted the plane and we ducked in under the clouds. They landed us at the airstrip at Caiguna and now it was up to us. Thanks guys.

Police were on hand, so we loaded up the highway patrol cars and off we headed.

The Briefing

On route we were briefed by the police.

There had been a storm with an immense amount of rain. As the plains out there are flat much of this water had run into a cave which acted much like a sink in your bathroom. According to the police this water had caused the mouth of the cave to fall in. Talking later to one of the people we rescued "there were rocks as big as caravans falling on us." There were 13 people trapped in the cave. No injuries were known. Our task was to get them out.

The Scene

We arrived to find a camp wrecked by torrential rain. Gear strewn over hundreds of metres, tarps in the top of trees and mud. Deep, slimy red mud, the type that sticks to the bottom of your boots and makes it hard to walk. Here, there were a couple of people who could brief us further. They were part of a documentary team who were diving in the underground rivers. They were using the cave as access and had gone several kilometres along this river so far. Most of it underwater. There were still 13 of their team trapped underground. The good news was they still had communications with them. I had never seen this type of communication set up. They had a huge loop of wire on the surface about 40 meters across and evidently the same underground directly below the top loop. This set up gave them a scratchy but readable signal, so we had communications with the trapped explorers.

The Rescue

There were a few trains of thought on how to get them out. The most popular for a while was to bring in a drill rig and drill a vertical shaft to the cave. The popularity declined as everyone debated how long it would take to get a rig in, drill the hole and the inherent dangers to those in the cave below. We could potentially cause the roof of the cave to fall in on them. It was decided we would attempt to clear the debris and get them out that way.

We started setting up a safe way to descend into the cave and clear the debris. After some time, it became evident this could take days so some of us were sent back to Cocklebiddy to try and get some sleep. Neil McCauley and I ended up in a motel unit that had been flooded by the storm. The floor was red with mud and water and the bedding was wet up to just below the mattress level. I think we managed to get a bit of sleep. Pretty soon we were woken up and told to get back to the cave. It was night-time.

When we got back, we learnt that Darren Brooks had found a way through the debris and would escort each trapped person out individually to the cave opening and we would get them to the surface. Each person appeared one by one over several hours. They were very grateful to be out of what they thought could have been a tomb for them. There were no serious injuries to any of us or the people we rescued. A good result all round.

We all congregated back at the Cocklebiddy pub where they put on free, everything for us. We could have drunk all night for free but by now we were all starting to get tired, the adrenalin had worn off and all we wanted was a shower and a sleep. Cocklebiddy motel was not suitable to sleep in, so we had to get back to Caiguna (about 120KMs) where there were dry motel units and hot showers.

20 Years Later

I have retired now. In March 2009, Phillip Petersen and I accompanied and directed by our wives were on a caravanning trip to Cape York. As we were crossing the Nullarbor Plain, I said to Phil, "How about we drop into the Pannikin Plains Cave and see what it looks like now."

Finding it was the first challenge.

Fortunately, the Cocklebiddy roadhouse has a mud map of some of the caves in the area. The cave didn't look much different, except that the debris has settled now, and it is dry and the sun shining.

It got me thinking though. All about the "what ifs"

What if we couldn't land the plane?

What if they were all deceased when we got there?

What if we couldn't get them out in time and we just had to wait for them to die?

What if we hadn't trained so hard and become such a close knitted team?

There are always lots of "what ifs" but this couldn't have turned out any better. All rescued safe, no injuries and a life experience which I found relatively easy to recall so I guess it has left a lasting imprint on my life.

When the others involved read this, I hope I have recounted it accurately on their behalf, but if there are discrepancies, I hope you remember I am 20 years older and a lot uglier with a fading memory.

Interesting Information

The movie "Sanctum" is based on the rescue of a group of researchers trapped in a Nullarbor cave at Pannikan Plains, near Cocklebiddy.

On that day there were thirteen cavers making a documentary on underwater diving in the cavern when there was a flash flood that rearranged rocks to form a blockage at the entrance.

They were trapped on the wrong side of the entrance however they were able to radio to five members of a ground crew who were outside the cave.

The State Emergency Service Cliff and Cave Rescue Team was activated and responded immediately.

The team consisted of Bob Coops (Team leader), Neil McCauly, Darren Brooks, Rod Ives and Jim Ridgwell.

The team got right into it and eventually a path was found and established by Darren Brooks. After many hours each of the researchers was brought to the surface. They had been trapped for nearly 36 hours.

The survivors, including Liz Wight, Jamie Hurworth and Dirk Spoffels from Sydney, were dragged out the main cave entrance after a huge pile of rubble and boulders had been removed by a team of rescuers, including 10 police and a dozen men from the Main Roads Department and the State Emergency Service.

They had been trapped for nearly 36 hours before being bought safely to the surface.

The Fire and Emergency Service Authority no longer supports the State Emergency Service Volunteers in the cave rescue role. This role is now performed by the Department of Environment and Conservation.

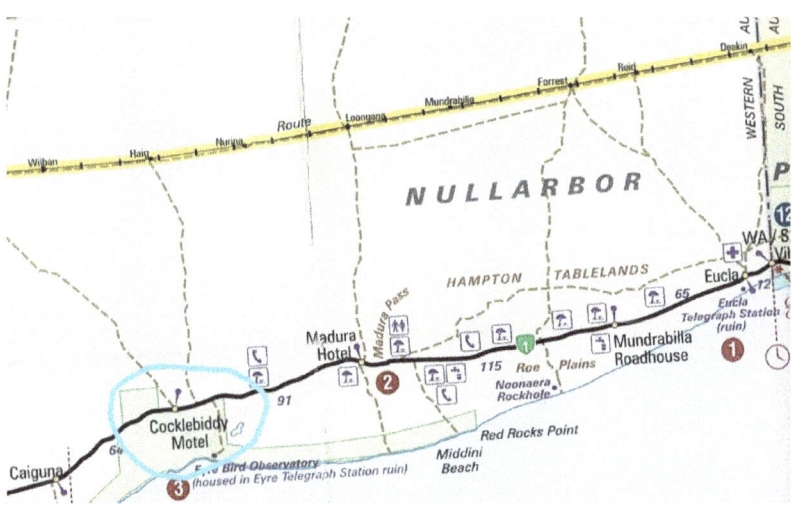

Map of the area – Pannikan Plains area is circled

1999 – Fremantle Tornado

On 13 August the State Emergency Service were called to an apartment block in Fremantle where a suspected tornado had hit and caused severe damage to a block of flats.

The Volunteers were able to clean up the debris and make the area safe pending building repairs.

1999 – The Robert Bogucki Search

In late July 1999 a tourist had gone missing in the desert. His camp site had been found, on the Pegasus track, and it appeared to be deserted for at least three days. There was a bike, backpack, water and small hutchie left there.

The police were alerted, and the search began.

The Derby and Broome State Emergency Service units were activated for a search.

The search was conducted for thirteen days and Mr Bogucki was not found.

The country was described as harsh and unrelenting. There were track and bush searches conducted. More than 10 heavy tyres were punctured or staked. Springs on several trailers were broken. Vehicles bogged in the fine sand. It was a nightmare for the Police and State Emergency Service Volunteers and Staff.

The McLarty track and associated areas were also searched.

Rotary winged and fixed wing aircraft joined the search.

From time to time footprints would be sited and then lost. Every lead draws a blank which led to all sort of campfire stories about his intentions.

The searchers knew the chances were slim however they did the best they could for thirteen days.

Mr Bogucki was eventually found alive and his story is amazing.

He had 3 days of food when he became lost. He lived off leaves and grasses for the other 37 days.

Mr Bogucki saw the planes and never realised they were looking for him. He had dug 3 metre holes to get water and then filled them in so animals wouldn't get trapped.

1999 – Moora Flood

Friday night 19 March 1999 saw the town of Moora carry on its business as usual even though they had had 2 days of relentless rain. It was continuous, but not heavy, and most people were able to carry on their normal activities.

Some water started to come up into the town on the Saturday at about 4.00pm and then slowed down. The last time there was a major flood in Moora was 1917.

By 8pm it was still raining, and the river had reached the top of its banks.

The State Emergency Service had been activated and teams of Volunteers from the Midlands Region Metropolitan Regions went to Moora to assist. About 10.00pm, the State Emergency Service came to town to monitor what was going on, but by 11.30pm, the rain stopped, and everyone went to bed, convinced it was just another State Emergency Service Red Alert.

In the early hours of Sunday morning at about 0120am, the Volunteers who were asleep on the motel room floor started to get wet and woke up.

The Volunteers and towns people awoke to the sound of dogs barking, the town fire siren wailing and to find the water quietly rising into their back yards. A number of people stepped out of their beds into knee-deep water that had already entered their houses. The phones eventually went out and all communications were cut.

The Hospital was evacuated as it was among the first to go under. Cars floated down the streets.

In the early hours of Sunday morning people began moving into the streets looking for high ground. The water was recorded as rising as much as 30 cm in 7 minutes.

On Sunday morning the town was frantic without communication and many children who had been on sleepovers came back to a closed town 5 feet deep in water

There were cattle trucks, front end loaders and super spreaders carrying people everywhere. Waves were made down the streets by these vehicles. These waves hit many fences, houses and even smashed some shop windows in the main street.

One of the first buildings to be inundated with water was the State Emergency Service headquarters.

The two high spots in the town were the Recreation Centre, and the High School. Both of these places were immediately turned into crises centres, with the front-end loaders sent to the supermarkets to get food for the people huddled in these two areas.

Buses arrived from Perth to take people to the Noalimba Reception Centre in Perth. This caused families to be split with the subsequent chaos.

On Monday the 22 March the full extent of the situation became apparent. Windows and walls were broken and there was mud everywhere. The town was closed to everybody except the Emergency Services and those people who were housed close by so they could take care of what was required

The State Emergency Service Staff and Volunteers had worked relentlessly on the Saturday night, the early hours of Sunday morning and continuously for 8 days to rescue people and their animals, resupply where required and assist during the mop up and recovery phase.

The rescues included helping people on and off the back of cattle trucks who were then relocated to safe areas.

This flood was caused by rain resulting from cyclone Elaine however, by the Thursday a further severe tropical Cyclone, Cyclone Vance, was advancing with fierce winds and pelting rain. All Monday and most of Tuesday was a frightening tense race against time to save whatever could be saved in Moora, however at the last-minute Cyclone Vance skirted Moora by 150 kms.

It was a time of devastation, but the community rallied together, and along with the generosity of businesses and the WA public, rebuilt the town.

1999 – Cyclone Vance

Severe Tropical Cyclone Vance formed on 19 March in the Timor Sea and moved towards the Pilbara coast. On 22 March it moved down the Exmouth Gulf causing winds in excess of 260kmh to severely damage or destroy many buildings in the town of Exmouth and to the south.

As there was advance warning of impending danger many people were evacuated from the town of Exmouth. There are no recorded fatalities and the damage estimate was in excess of $100m.

The effects of TC Vance were felt in a number of places with storm surge flooding a number of houses in Onslow, roads being washed out, dust storms and more than 50,000 people losing their power.

The State Emergency Service (part of FESA) was activated and had a team of Staff and more than 20 Volunteers stationed in the town for 2 weeks doing recovery and clean-up work.

2001 – Kiwirrkurra Flooding and Relocation

Kiwirrkurra is a small community in Western Australia in the Gibson Desert, 1,200 km east of Port Hedland and 850 km west of Alice Springs.

It was established around a bore in the early 1980s as a Pintupi (western desert) outstation and became a permanent community in 1983. It was one of the last areas with nomadic Aboriginals who lived a traditional life, with little change from centuries past. They lived a migratory life, surviving as hunters and gatherers in the desert rich in food and other resources – the last of the desert people.

In early 2000 the community, being in a low-lying area without drainage, was flooded. Further flooding occurred in early March 2001. This second flood caused inundated of the dwellings and community buildings.

The State Emergency Service in the Pilbara/Kimberley region became involved and conducted an evacuation of its population of 170 persons, first briefly to Kintore and then to the Norforce base in Alice Springs.

The State Emergency Management Committee (SEMC) met to decide what they could do about the situation. The SEMC appointed Regional Director Gordon Hall, reporting to FESA CEO Bob Mitchell, to build a temporary community for the 200 Kiwirrkurra people at Moropoi, (a station near Niagara Dam north east of Menzies) and relocate the displaced persons from the military base in the Northern Territory. This was to be completed within 14 days.

The team was established and included Gordon Hall (leader), Les Watkins, Mike Breen, Francis Mott, Colin Brown (Kalgoorlie) and Barry Jones (based at Alice Springs for the operation).

Contractors were employed to supply accommodation units and a meeting place was established.

Three elders were bought to Moropoi from Alice Springs. A number of bush meetings were conducted, and the elders advised on a number of matters.

The evacuees spent 4 weeks at the Norforce base in Alice Springs.

The Moropoi Community took 14 days to complete. All the persons were transported by Boeing 737 aircraft and buses. The aircraft were only available after National Jet had finished the east west run at midnight. They had to be back on the tarmac in Perth by 530am for the morning run to the east. Two trips were made, 2 days apart arriving in Alice Springs at 2.30am. The planes then flew to Kalgoorlie and the community members were transported by bus to Moropoi. Kalgoorlie SES Volunteers provided support at the Kalgoorlie airport during the debarkation of the community members.

On the fourteenth day the community at Moropoi was handed over to the Department of Family and Children's Services.

2004 – Boxing Day Tsunami

The most significant tsunami was on Boxing Day 2004 when a 9.1 magnitude quake struck off the northern tip of Sumatra in Indonesia.

Scientists say that this was the third largest earthquake ever recorded. It lasted up to ten minutes and caused the earth to vibrate up to 3cm.

More than 30 cubic kilometres of water was displaced which resulted in a massive tsunami across the Indian Ocean

About 230 000 people were killed across 14 countries.

On the Western Australia coast there was quite an affect.

There was a draw down and subsequent wave at Mersey Point, Rockingham. Around 25 people were crossing the sand bar to Penguin Island when the wave came back and washed the people off the bar and into the sea. They were all rescued and survived.

Snorkelers in Geographe Bay ran out of water, many beach goers ended up with wet towels as waves washed up onto beaches and 20 centimetres of water passed down Marine Terrace in Geraldton.

Pleasure boats in Thomson Bay, Rottnest Island, bounced around hitting the sea grasses on the bottom of the ocean.

There were many other reports along the coast, however there were no reported injuries or serious damage.

2006 Tsunami – Steep Point WA

In July 2006 an earthquake in the ocean off Java caused a small tsunami to hit the shores at Steep Point in WA. There were 55 campers there that night and there were three waves with the second being the largest.

It was close to low tide when there was a loud roar heard just before the tsunami arrived.

One camp was destroyed however nobody was injured.

Sand dunes were eroded, and sand redeposited on the road.

Geoscience Australia sent scientists to Steep Point to do several digs in the area and gather scientific material as part of their studies.

Other Tsunami Affecting WA

There is a lot of anecdotal and other evidence of tsunami affecting the Western Australian coast.

Below is an excerpt from a letter found in the Onslow Museum during the research for Tsunami effects along the WA coastline. It was written in Nanutarra on 16 September 1883.

> *"The most startling news we have is that we have had a shock of an earthquake, also a tidal wave. The sheep were just being landed from the Laughing Wave when it took place and one of the dingys* (sic) *was swamped while another was washed up high and dry, sheep and all. 12 sheep were drowned out of the dingy swamped. The noise was heard all over the district and we have heard also in the south."*

In August 1883, Krakatoa, an island in the Strait of Sunda, erupted causing an estimated death toll of 36,000. The sound, subsequent tremors and tsunami affected many parts of the world.

There is evidence of other tsunami affecting the coast of WA including the Exmouth area.

2005 – Perth May Storms

The State Emergency Service received advice that a significant event, in the form of a severe cold front, was moving towards Perth.

Four days later on 15 May, the Coordination Centre was set up at the bunker in Belmont, in preparation for widespread damage and calls for assistance.

At 6am 16 May the severe cold front crossed the cost. Several mini tornadoes (technically microbursts) formed on the leading edge of the front and were reported from Bicton and Bunbury. Other possible mini-tornadoes or severe winds affected the suburbs of Maddington, Martin and Roleystone; Hope Valley to Serpentine; Westfield, Kelmscott and Clifton Hills; Toodyay, Australind and Bokal (near Darkin).

Cars were pushed from one lane to another on the Kwinana Freeway as the mini-tornadoes crossed the river.

In Perth the most serious damage was to a primary school in Bicton and a house that was demolished in an adjacent street. Other damage included several roofs that were completely lifted off and a significant amount of tree, fence and roof tile damage.

More than 100,000 homes were reported to have lost power during the event.

In Bunbury a mini-tornado caused a trail of damage along the main street of the CBD. The most significant damage was the destruction of the rear section of the ABC studio as a result of a falling crane. Businesses along the main street were badly damaged with 3 or 4 older buildings unable to be repaired. The Bunbury High School was also closed following building damage.

The State Emergency Service activated rescue teams and more than 2,000 calls for assistance were received.

2010 – Perth Hailstorm

Severe thunderstorms occurred on the afternoon and evening of Monday 22 March causing large hail, heavy rain and severe winds that resulted in damage estimated in the several hundreds of millions of dollars. This storm produced the largest hail known to have occurred in Perth. This storm was one of the costliest natural disasters in Perth's history with damage estimates in excess of $700m.

The storm was the most significant weather event since the May 1994 windstorm.

The rainfall in Mt Lawley was 40.2 mm which was the fifth highest daily rainfall for March on record for the official Perth site. The largest recorded hail occurred in Perth's western and northern suburbs. Hail stones 5 to 6 cm in diameter were measured in a number of areas including Wembley, Crawley, Nedlands, Shenton Park, Subiaco and Floreat. Many other areas report hail with some as big as golf balls.

More than 150,000 properties were without power at the peak of the storm.

There were widespread reports of property damage caused by rain, strong winds and hail.

Twenty people had to be evacuated from the emergency department at Joondalup Hospital in Perth's northern suburbs after parts of the ceiling caved in.

The storm's trail of destruction extended from Joondalup down through the western suburbs and further south to Mandurah.

Flights in and out of Perth as well as metropolitan train and bus services were disrupted.

More than 100 people had to be evacuated from an apartment block on Mounts Bay Road near King's Park in Perth's CBD after the storm caused a landslide.

Affected suburbs included Rockingham, Orelia, Baldivis, Waikiki, Medina, Cooloongup, Wilson, Hillman, Maida Vale, High Wycombe, Bicton, Mosman Park, Clarkson, Girrawheen and Currambine.

A block of units in Harrison Street, Rockingham had its roof blown off.

A school in Kewdale sustained major damage when the roof blew off one of the buildings.

Other homes received internal water damage, and some householders reported broken windows and fallen fences.

In Waroona, south of Perth, many calls were received with reports of fallen trees, powerlines and fences. The South Western Highway was closed in the area due to storm damage and debris.

The State Emergency Service received more than 3,000 calls for assistance and the volunteers responded throughout the night and subsequent days to effect temporary repairs or help community members.

2010 – Carnarvon Flooding

The town of Carnarvon was hit by its worst flooding in 50 years that year and the main town was cut off.

Carnarvon town goes through floods regularly (typically about every 5 years) and the town is saved from devastation by a serious of levy banks that have been installed around the main part of town.

Helicopters were called in that year to rescue people from rooftops after a monsoonal low dumped over 245mm of rain on Carnarvon. This rain constituted 20mm more than the yearly average.

Families were flooded out of their homesteads on isolated inland stations, and at the Gascoyne Junction outpost, water rose to the top of buildings. A police helicopter winched 19 people from the roofs of the pub and other buildings.

The normally dry Gascoyne River broke its banks as water rushed towards Carnarvon, where it reached a height of 7.9m.

During the town's previous worst flood, in 1960, the river rose to 7.61m.

Plantations around Carnarvon were devastated by the floods with many crops and roads destroyed.

The State Emergency Service was activated and carried out many rescues, welfare checks, resupplies and continual updates to residents on the progress and height of the flood waters.

2014 - The Search for the Missing Aircraft - MH370

Malaysia Airlines Flight MH370 was an international passenger flight operated by Malaysia Airlines that disappeared on 8 March 2014 while flying from Kuala Lumpur International Airport, Malaysia, to Beijing Capital International Airport in China.

The aircraft had last made voice contact with air traffic control at around 1am (WAT) 8 March when it was over the South China Sea. This was less than an hour after take-off.

MH370 disappeared from air traffic controllers' radar screens shortly afterwards. Malaysian military radar continued to track the aircraft as it deviated westwards from its planned flight path and crossed the Malay Peninsula.

The aircraft, a Boeing 777-200ER, was carrying 12 Malaysian crew members and 227 passengers from 15 nations.

Analysis of satellite communications between the aircraft and Inmarsat's satellite communications network concluded that the flight continued until at least 08:19 and flew south into the southern Indian Ocean.

Although the precise location could not be determined, Australia took charge of the search on 17 March, when the search moved to the southern Indian Ocean.

The final phase of the search, the largest and most expensive in aviation history, was a comprehensive survey of the sea floor about 1,800 kilometres south-west of Perth, Western Australia. This began in October 2014.

Nothing was found of the aircraft until 29 July 2015, when a piece of marine debris, later confirmed to be a flaperon from Flight MH 370, washed ashore on La Réunion Island.

Dedicated and professional Volunteers of the State Emergency Service from WA and the rest of Australia, both as Air Search Observers (ASO) and Ground Crew, swung into action. They worked tirelessly throughout the above operation flying many missions across the Southern Indian Ocean.

There were 138 SES Volunteers, 12 DFES staff and 2 AMSA staff involved in the roles of Air Search. The SES Ground Crews came from CSU and Bayswater whilst the SES Volunteers Association provided the Volunteer

Liaison Officers. These numbers included SES Volunteers from other Australian jurisdictions; 4 from SA, 4 from the NT, 4 from Qld, 8 from Tasmania, 8 from the ACT, 9 from NSW and 12 from Victoria.

Further to this, DFES provide a total of 12 staff as ground support and Air Search Observers.

WA Air observers about to board the plane (photo G Hall)

Air observers from the Northern Territory Emergency Service (in Blue)

(photo G Hall)

Chapter 17 - History of Some SES Units

The SES history in WA would not be complete without a snapshot of how SES Units have evolved at local level. The following are contributions about various SES Units, as well as past and present members.

Albany State Emergency Service

The Albany State Emergency Service was established in 1982 when the Regional SES Coordinator at the time John Umney approached the Local Army Reserve Unit Cadre Staff WO2 D Cook with an idea that some of the Reserve members could put their skills to use in serving the community, with WO2 Cook being the First Albany SES Local Manager.

From there several Reserve Members joined the newly formed Albany SES Unit bringing with them a wealth of experience. One of these members Gary Logan went to Mt Macedon and completed a Mass Rescue Instructor Qualification. In the initial years the roles of Search and Storm were put to good use and Albany SES was given the additional role of Cliff and Cave Rescue, a skill that has been used a frequently on the coast and around the Great Southern Region.

The Albany SES Unit started with its headquarters in a two-story house and soon outgrew that facility, to then progressing to where the Albany Unit is currently located in an old Girl Guides building with additional sheds for vehicles, trailers and equipment.

Over the years there has been a steady stream of dedicated volunteers that epitomise the ethos of 'We Serve' in the community with some of those taking on major roles within FESA/DFES including Gary Logan and Tim Dalwood.

The list of Local Managers/Coordinators include WO2 D Cook, Rene Vermuelen, John Hallet, Andy Roberts, Murray Clark, Ron Panting, Joanne Weekes, Tim Dalwood, Kenneth Pascho, Peter McMahon, Sheryn Prior, Nigel De Snoo and Kate Russell (2020). Ron Panting served the longest term as Local Manager with around 13 years in the role and also received the

Peter Keillor Award for achievement, excellence and enthusiasm as a Volunteer.

Armadale State Emergency Service

The Armadale Local Volunteer Emergency Service (LVES) group was formed on 30th January 1964 in the Armadale Lesser Hall with Des Franklin nominated as the Controller. The volunteers wore blue Civil Defence type overalls with section badges, hard hats and army boots. The group was also provided with a lot of equipment, including personal dosimeters, which would have been used in the case of a nuclear attack as Armadale was on the periphery of the range of nuclear attack on Perth and the Kwinana industrial site.

A lot of training was undertaken including visits to the Old Fighter Squadron in the underground base at Belmont, which we now call the Bunker. Two Armadale LVES Volunteers were lucky to do some specialist training at Mount Macedon in Victoria.

In the early years all the stores and equipment were held at the St John Ambulance Depot, then it was moved the Metro Bus Depot until it was relocated to under the grandstand of the Gwynne Park Oval to a very old house on Champion Drive until 1985 when the Armadale SES moved into a newly constructed facility at 53 Owen Road where a major upstairs extension to add a training room and offices was completed in 2010.

The volunteers have been deployed to many incidents over many decades including for Cyclone Tracey evacuee reception in 1974 at Perth Airport; major flooding in Moora, Queensland and Adelaide; Tropical Cyclones in Broome, Port Hedland, Carnarvon, Karratha and Queensland; Severe Storms in Melbourne, Waroona and Bunbury; many Land Searches and in particular those at Byford, Billabong, Fitzroy Crossing, Menzies, Albany, Stirling Ranges, Pemberton, Nannup plus Air Searches near Bunbury, Christmas Island, Cocos Island, Port Hedland and searching for Abbey Sunderland near Africa, as well as support during major fires in Boddington, Esperance, Kalgoorlie, Hyden and Norseman.

The following is an approximate list of controllers, coordinators and local managers with the times they served:

The first group controller was Des Franklin 1964 – 1974. James Garrett was Local Coordinator 1980 – 1984, then Mike Davis 1985 – 1994, Paul Manning 1994 – 1997. Debbie Jackson was appointed Local Manager 1997 – 2000, then Herman Hofman 2000 – 2012, Peter Clark 2013 – 2016, with Connie Eikelboom appointed Local Manager in 2016.

Bassendean State Emergency Service Unit

The Bassendean State Emergency Service had its first meeting on 14th December 1983. The archives room under the council chambers was the meeting place and with ingenuity this was turned into the first SES Emergency Operations Centre.

Like many State Emergency Service units there was a need relating to response to natural hazard events in the local community. Bassendean lies in the Swan River Flood Plain with many homes vulnerable to flooding.

The unit gradually collected equipment which was supplied by the Commonwealth, the State Government and the Bassendean Town Council. One of the milestones in the unit's development was the presentation of the WASES supplied Toyota 4-wheel drive vehicle. The Mayer, John Cox, presented the vehicle to the unit on 19th October 1985.

In 1987 the new headquarters facility was opened at the current location on the corner of Scadden and Troy St where it is co-located with the Town of Bassendean Works Depot. This proved to be a far better alternate to the archives room.

The Bassendean unit had the flood rescue boat role until 2016. Their flood rescue jet boat was deployed to the Moora floods in 1999 and also utilised for large public events where safety near or on the water was of concern including the Australia Day fireworks

The Bassendean SES Local Coordinator from 1983 – 1985 was Peter Gilberthorpe. Clive Abel was Local Coordinator/Manager 1985 – 2001. Gordon Munday was appointed Local Manager 2001 – 2019 with Stephen Blackford appointed Local Manager in 2019.

Bayswater State Emergency Service Unit

A contribution written in late 1986:

"SES Bayswater was formed in November 1971 with the approval of the then Shire of Bayswater with the inaugural meeting being held on 28th February 1972. The Unit moved into their first premises, formerly an Infant Health Centre, in Toowong Street in October 1972.

Membership is currently 24 including Administration, Rescue and Welfare. Although many members have come and gone over the years, three names continue to appear. They are John Pickles, Lesley Brokensha and Harry James. All three take part in the unit's operation. Current equipment includes 1 issue 4WD, 2 trailers, 7 ton mobile command post and store, truck mounted cherry picker and a 4WD fire/rescue unit.

Bayswater Coordinator is Frank Obrecht, who is Ground Maintenance Supervisor with Hooker Rex."

Local Managers (Coordinators) since the 1980s include Frank Obrecht, Ray Mahony, Glenn Hall, Tracy Barker, Andrae Moore and Nichola Wilkinson. Alan Hawke is currently acting in the role of Local Manager.

Past Local Manager and unit member Glenn Hall is currently a District Officer with DFES.

Boddington State Emergency Service Unit

Prior to the formation of the Boddington SES unit in 1979 there was a small Civil Defence trailer stored in the local shire council workshop that contained Hobb nail British army boots, Overalls and lots of heavy 35mm manila rope, heavy steel pulley blocks, gas masks and lots of army webbing, crow bars, canvas stretchers and world war 2 first aid kits and water bottles on webbing belts.

Wayne English was contacted by the then South West Regional Coordinator for the WA State Emergency Service Mr Nial Wilmot seeking interested community volunteers to establish an SES unit in Boddington. There was a particular need for a Road Accident Rescue capable unit in the area. Wayne and two other Boddington locals decided to form the Boddington SES Unit and 41 years on, Wayne is still coordinating and managing the activities of the Boddington SES Unit.

The Unit originally operated out of what was then the old Shire office building alongside the workshop which was a very small two room building with no kitchen and toilet facilities. The construction of a new headquarters was completed in 1998 to effectively run and further develop the Unit. The new office building was attached to the shed building which was the former Boddington Shire council workshop building.

This contribution is evident in the fact that as of 2020 we currently have, and this is from the original three members in 1979

The Boddington SES Unit has transformed into a very professional SES Unit from its humble beginnings of 3 Volunteers to 17 Volunteers with a broad range of skills and experience ready to respond to its prime of Road Accident Rescue within an area of coverage totalling about 1000 km of highways and major arterial roads. Unit Volunteers also respond to storm damage call outs and land searches as well as support to fire incidents.

In 2003 the Unit designed a Road Crash Rescue crew cab truck that was acquired solely by Unit fund raising. Since the advent of ESL funding and much improved fleet vehicles (which DFES has designed with the involvement of experienced volunteers) life has gotten a little easier, although Volunteers still have the 24/7 000 calls for Road Crash Rescue call-outs for everything from cars verses trees, kangaroos, trucks, road trains verses cars verses road trains and a couple of plane crashes in the area.

Wayne English was the inaugural Local Coordinator and remains the appointed Local Manager of Boddington SES.

Bridgetown State Emergency Service

The Bridgetown SES was established in 1989 following the publication of an article in the local paper which had been placed by the Shire council seeking volunteers interested in starting an SES unit.

While there wasn't an actual incident that triggered the Units establishment, local planning would have identified risks that warranted an SES unit with trained Volunteers, able to respond in either a combat or a support role. SES was a division of Police at the time and initial meetings were conducted at the old police station followed by the new police station.

SES meetings and training were conducted at the old Drive-In kiosk, until the Unit moved to its present location in Civil St. This building had an upgrade recently.

The Local Co-ordinators/Managers over the 31 years include Ken Web, Colin Jeffery, Lindsay Rayson, Peter Ditrich, Ann O'Keefe and Paul Hegney.

Bunbury State Emergency Service

The Bunbury Unit of the SES started with its first meeting on 22 November 1962 in the Technical School building in Arthur Street, in the CBD. Its first title was the Bunbury Volunteer Emergency Service (VES) or Civil Defence, in some correspondence.

In 1966 it as moved to a three-bedroom asbestos and tin built as a pre-apprentice carpenter project home in Ecclestone Street Carey park. This was the Unit's home until 2017. When the local traffic police were subsumed into the State Police department, in the true volunteering form, the VES Unit 'stole' their now dis-used vehicle inspection shed next door. So now they could acquire vehicles and equipment, which was then shifted from a Regional Store, into the Bunbury shed.

Not long afterward, the Unit raised the considerable funding required to modify the 3-bedroom home and strapped on the nail bags. The work was done in the mid 80's to change the internal lay-out to provide an Operations Centre, Communication Centre and a commercial kitchen, along with a training room. This facility was now more suited to the purpose of an Emergency Operations Centre.

In 2016, the Unit was successful in gaining a$1.4M LGGS grant, to ditch the asbestos and build a 'real' LEOC. Subsequently, the Unit moved into its new, purpose-built home in February of 2017. It is now situated at 11 Clement Street in the Halifax industrial centre, in the south-east of town.

Bunbury continues to have a strong membership, with over 60 regular members. Training is weekly with it not unusual to have two weekend courses held at the Bunbury LHQ per month. The Unit membership is proudly able to claim equal male and female membership. There is also a strong social fabric within the Unit and a strong family focus. In 2015, the Unit was awarded the SES Team Award at the Annual FES Conference

Awards Presentation. The Unit was recognised for its restructure that was undertaken to change our operating paradigm from the 70's to a more focussed business model to help us cope with the increasing administration load. The Unit continues to operate two command streams, Administration and Logistics and Operations Command groups. This model is still suiting us well, with another study being conducted to further streamline our effectiveness.

The Unit is regularly called upon to assist the Regional HQ with various functions such as administration support during major incidents, communication support, ground support and incident management team staff for significant fires and the Unit HQ houses the Regional ICV. Several Unit members are also joint crew for the team. The Unit also has a number of VR technicians, making up the bulk of the Regional team and houses and maintains the Regional VR Trailer.

Significant emergencies that Bunbury Unit members have attended include the 1964 floods in East Bunbury, 1978 TC Alby, Blackwood River floods of February 1982, Gracetown cliff collapse in September 1996, Bunbury tornado 2005, Australind tornado in 2007, Several resupply operations to the Kimberly Region, South Bunbury tornado 2007, Team members participated in 2 NDRC teams and assisted with the hosting of the event held in Bunbury in 2007, Melbourne hailstorm 2008, TC Yasi in Queensland, several campaign fires in the Goldfields, Esperance, Carnarvon and Lower South West Regions, the significant storms in Bunbury and surrounds (450 RFA) in 2012, including a strike Team from Bunbury being sent to a TC in Carnarvon and the South Australian Storm event in 2015.

The earliest Local Managers (Coordinators) for Bunbury were Les D'Vorak (Snr) in the mid to late 70's, followed by Ray Hall, John Thornborough, Ian Axell and the current Manager is Chris Widmer ESM.

Busselton State Emergency Service

The Busselton Unit was established around 1967 with Civil Defence type equipment consisting of a few stretchers, some blankets, a few lengths of natural fibre rope and two 27Mhz Pony radios which operated from torch batteries. These items were housed in a storage shed at the rear of the Shire offices.

Few people had heard of the Local Volunteer Emergency Service (LVES), as it was then known. Formal meetings were held only annually, with little activity occurring between meetings, which were held in the library of the Primary School. Equipment consisted of a few stretchers, some blankets, a few lengths of rope and two 27MHz Pony radios, which operated from torch batteries. These items we housed in a storage shed at the rear of the Shire offices.

Nevertheless, interest grew, meetings became more frequent, until that great day when a small building was transported to a corner of the Shire Depot yard and re-erected for out use. Then came the new vehicle, trailer, radios and all the other equipment.

Through the 1980s meetings and training nights were held regularly, membership grew and the guys and girls in orange overalls started to become recognized and respected in the community. But as an organization grown, it becomes more ambitious and we were really not happy. Our headquarters was much too small, and the centre of a light industrial area is hardly the best location for an HF radio station! The Shire Council was sympathetic, but could offer no alternative, so we carried on as we were for around ten years.

Suddenly, out of the blue, came good news beyond our wildest dreams! The Water Authority was moving to new premises, and their old headquarters was offered to the Shire at a peppercorn rental for some community-based organization and we were the successful applicants. The site consisted of a large area of land – more than adequate for any possible future requirements and numerous buildings in fair condition. It was obvious that much work and money would be needed to transform open machinery sheds into the type of buildings we required. This was a more suitable area for the Busselton SES to operate from and grow to the large successful unit that it is today.

The earliest Local Managers (Coordinators) included Tes Hunt during the 1980s, Ken Pember and Adrian De Kleer. The current Local Manager is Wayne Credaro. There have been others who have held the position of Local Manger and many volunteers passing through the unit.

Past Local Coordinator, Adrian De Kleer is currently a District Officer with DFES.

Canning - South Perth State Emergency Service Unit

The Canning-South Perth State Emergency Service started as the Canning SES in 1984. At this time, the unit was located in the Canning Town Hall in George Street, Cannington and then later transferred to the old Post Office Building on the corner of Albany Highway and Ashburton Street, Cannington. The unit used this building as their headquarters for about 10 years, however, as there was no parking it caused logistical problems with the unit vehicles having to be collected then returned each training night between the headquarters and the Canning Depot. Equipment equally had to be stored offsite in a storeroom on Ashburton Street. In 1994 the Canning SES moved to premises built for the Unit at the Canning Depot which is where the unit is still co-located with council workers today.

In the early 1990's the City of South Perth joined to support the unit with the provision of additional finance and a new rescue vehicle. The unit's name was then changed to Canning South Perth SES. Between 2004-2005 the unit's premises were extended and then fitted out to provide space to house the flood boats and a reconnaissance vehicle which were previously stored outside in the weather.

Some of the significant events that the unit have been involved in include the South Perth Tornado (1995), flood rescue operations for the Moora Floods (1999), the Exmouth Cyclone Vance (1999), aerial search for sailor Abby Sunderland (2010), Perth Hail Storm (2010), and bush fire support for the Perth Hills Fires (2014) and the Waroona Fires (2016).

Today the unit plays an active role with its leadership, trainers and members skilled and active in many SES skills including flood search and rescue, air observation and storm damage operations.

Local Coordinators/Managers include Larry Lawrence from 1984 until 1987, Rod Ives until 1988, Valerie Donovan until 1990, Brian Gorton until 1992, Rodney Paterson until 1993, Harry Finlay until 1997, Fiona Paterson until 2000, Michael Lalor until 2004, Peter Austin until 2007, William (Tony) Brown 2013, Andrew Bray until 2019 and currently David Reed (2020).

Carnarvon State Emergency Service Unit

The Carnarvon State Emergency Service Unit has always played a strategic role due to its isolation on the WA coast about 900km north of Perth. It lies on a river delta system at the mouth of the Gascoyne River and is a major supplier for fruit and vegetables for WA.

The Carnarvon SES like most units started out with a Civil Defence role which became more significant with the establishment of the Harold E Holt Communications Station on the North West Cape which was thought to be a potential nuclear target in the 1960s.

In the early years, equipment was stored in a Carnarvon Shire shed and emergency operations were run out of the old Shire Hall in Francis Street or the old facility in Robinson Street known locally as "The Woolshed".

In 1982 a cyclone rated headquarters was built in Carnarvon where the Carnarvon SES Headquarters co-located with the WASES Regional Headquarters. It was the first of its kind to be built in WA and it was designed to operate as a control and coordination centre for the whole north west of WA. The Carnarvon SES still operates out of this facility in Camel Lane.

Over the decades SES Volunteers have respond to coastal cliff rescues, land and air searches, cyclones and flood emergencies, among a range of other support roles. Major flooding of the Gascoyne River occurs on average about every five years and most significantly in the early 1960s, 1980, 1995 and 2010. Significant operations have included:

- Cyclone Hazel 1978 which did significant damage to the jetty at Cape Cuvier and caused millions of dollars damage to the Gascoyne/Shark Bay region.
- Cyclone Herbie (May 1988) when the bulk carried "Korean Star" run aground near Cape Cuvier. The Carnarvon unit rescued the crew members from the ship during very hazardous conditions.
- Cyclone Bobby (February 1995) when the cyclone initially posed no great threat to Carnarvon, however the subsequent flooding of the Gascoyne River resulted in the Carnarvon SES unit putting in 924-man hours and answering 1,300 phone calls for assistance.
- The 2010 Gascoyne River flood is regarded as the most severe flood to take place along the Gascoyne River. In a 24-hour period on 17 December, 247 mm of rain fell in the catchment area causing

widespread damage in the region. Property damage was estimated at $100 million.
- Cyclone Olwyn (2015) was the most significant tropical cyclone to affect the Gascoyne coast in decades, causing severe damage to houses as well as the town's water and power facilities. The area was without water and electricity supplies for several days and the entire banana crop was destroyed.

Over the years there have been many volunteers dedicating themselves to serving the Carnarvon community. Local Volunteer Bernie McNamara ESM became WASES Regional Coordinator – Gascoyne Murchison based in Carnarvon, before transferring to Perth as the WASES Regional Manager – Metropolitan South and later, the FESA District Officer – SES Metropolitan South.

The list of Carnarvon SES Local Co-ordinators includes Bernie McNamara ESM and Kevin Burkett. The Carnarvon SES Local Managers list includes Kaye Lawry, Ernie Reynolds, Michael Stroet, Russell Bartels and currently Elsa Alston.

Cockburn State Emergency Service Unit

The City of Cockburn Voluntary State Emergency Service officially commenced in December 1981 with 6 members growing to 23 in February 1982 with Oleg Milosaljevic appointed as the first Local Coordinator.

Council provided a house in Spearwood as the first base for the Unit with equipment supplied by WASES and a secondhand Land rover 4wd Station Wagon purchased with donated the funds. In June 1983 the Unit relocated to the old Council Parks & Garden Depot in Kent Street, Spearwood, however it wasn't until the completion of significant modifications by the Volunteers in February, 1988 that the Kent Street building was officially opened by the then Mayor of Cockburn, Mr Don Miguel. Membership by then had grown to 40. The Unit stayed in these very ad hoc premises until the Cockburn Emergency Services building in Buckley Street, Cockburn was completed in September 2012 where the Unit is currently co-located with the South Coogee Bushfire Brigade.

It wasn't until late 1988 that the Unit could afford the purchase and operational expense of an initial 7 pagers which were circulated on a weekly basis to Rescue Team members to activate them in call out situations. It sped up the old process of having to ring individual members on their landlines – no mobile phones then!

The implementation of the Emergency Services Levy in 2001 took the pressure off members to fundraise for much needed equipment not provided by WASES & FESA and allowed them to concentrate on fully training and operational duties.

During the 39 years of operation there have been many activations of the Unit – some almost overwhelming by their magnitude such as the May 1994 storms where the Unit alone received over 300 calls for assistance. Others had a profound impact - notably the searches for both Jamie Godden and Gerard Ross in 1997 where sadly these young boys had met with foul play.

Oleg Milosaljevic remained Unit Manager until the end of 1992 followed by Robert Hopkins, Robert Odgers, Brendan Bradley, Keith Drayton (twice), Enrico di Russo, Michael Mullins, Drew Devereux, Steve Wells and currently Ian Dury.

Gnowangerup State Emergency Service Unit

Local Police officer Neil Warner was the person who initiated the formation of the Gnowangerup State Emergency Service Unit in 1989. Prior to this it was a Civil Defence Unit. The Unit was founded as a result of a call for searchers to locate a severely injured Cub/Scout Leader on Mount Trio in the Stirling Ranges in the Shire of Gnowangerup located the Great Southern Region of Western Australia.

The early years of training and operations was based in an old Homes West house occupied previously by the Department of Social Security in Bell Street, Gnowangerup.

After many years in premises that were very cramped and unsuitable for task, a new purpose-built facility was erected and opened in May 2016 on the original site in Bell Street.

The unique thing about this small rural based unit is their proud history from 1989 to current day when the unit has never failed to respond to a request for assistance from DFES, FESA, WASES or the Police.

Local Coordinators/Local Managers since the unit was established include Neil Warner, Ray Peucker, John Ackermans, Andrew Myers, Eddie Seaman, Peter Blows and currently Les Nayda.

Kalamunda State Emergency Service Unit

The Kalamunda Civil Defence and Emergency Services group was born in October 1963 and met monthly in a room at the rear of the Kalamunda Agricultural Hall. In 1968 the unit moved to an old house next to the Shire Offices in Canning Road (this house was later demolished to make way for the Jack Healy Senior Citizens Centre).

It is believed that the unit disbanded in 1970/71 with some moves made to reform the unit in 1973, however it was not until 1978 that the unit as we know it today came into existence.

Meetings of the Kalamunda Local Volunteer Emergency Service were held in a room shared with the Bushfire Service at the rear of the old Shire office building, Canning Rd, Kalamunda. The vehicles and trailers were parked in a double garage adjacent to the building.

The Kalamunda SES Unit moved into a new purpose built co-located SES/BFS headquarters at 42 Raymond Road Walliston in 1991.

Kalamunda unit has responded to Severe Storm, Local Flooding, Land and Air Search and Fire Fighting support locally and at locations throughout WA and the eastern states. Significant events include the loss of the Kalamunda Library roof during a storm and support at a Fireworks Factory explosion.

Local Co-ordinators/Managers over the years include- Richard Price, Colin Ainsworth, Neville Armitage, Richard Maslen, Derek Fletcher (1991 -1996 and 2000-2006) Bruce McLennan, Chris Kin-Maung, Andrew Carter, John White, Arthur Hutchinson (retired May 2016), Cynthia Paterson and currently Warwick Martindale.

The Unit's most celebrated member is a former local businessman, who was also a Shire Councillor and Chief Bush Fire Control Officer, Local Manager Derek Fletcher OAM who also received the 2001 Centenary of Australia Medal. Derek also served as a FESA District Manager before retiring to the coast. Past Local Manager Chris Kin-Maung is a current DFES District Officer.

Karratha State Emergency Service Unit

The Karratha SES unit was born out of the requirement of the remote and isolated community to have some sort of coordination for a number of emergency events including, search, road crash rescue, cyclone impact response and cyclone community preparation.

The beginning of the Karratha SES unit can be traced back to the late 1960's, where for many years it worked in a fragmented manner. As recently as 1985 it operated from the local police station with the communication centre being located within the Water Authority, in a borrowed office, whilst its equipment was housed in a number of areas around Karratha. The training also occurred at various venues.

The appointment in 1987 of a new Deputy Coordinator, Lyn Rankin, saw the first injection of an attempt to pull all sections together and to bring the unit back online with regard to Training and Administration. Encouraged by Roebourne Shire Councillor, Ben Sharpe, and with significant input by Lyn Rankin, 1986 saw the emergence of plans for an emergency service headquarters.

In 1987 construction of a new headquarters building (with no windows) commenced in Balmoral Rd and was occupied in February 1988. The headquarters still serves the unit well today after more than 30 years of use.

The Karratha Unit have been activated for numerous tropical cyclones, floods and fire related responses, not just in the Pilbara but also in the adjoining Kimberley and Gascoyne/Murchison areas. The Unit has responded to countless rescues due to road crash and in the Karijini Gorges, as well as countless land searches and performed many hundreds of hours in aircraft as air observers or drop masters. The Unit also provided a catering team during the 1990's that would travel to wherever there be a requirement, regardless of the location.

The Karratha SES Road Crash Rescue Team represented WA at the Annual National Challenge of Australasian Road Rescue Organisation in 2007, held in Perth.

Up until 1988, the OIC Karratha Police was the SES Local Coordinator, followed by Lyn Rankin until 1989, Robert Te until 1996, Steve Cable ESM until 2007 and currently Trevor Patton ESM.

There have been many Volunteers passing through this unit including Robert Te who took on a role within WASES/FESA as a District Manager.

Kununurra State Emergency Service unit

Extract from the Book, *Kununurra-From Dreams to Reality by Keith Wright & Norma Wainwright;* contributed by former Local Managers Lincoln Heading and John Hobbs.

The original concept leading to the development of the unit was the appointment of a Local Co-ordinator in early 1970. At that time, it was known as the Civil Defence and Emergency Service.

In about 1978 a state-wide radio communications network was developed with the installation of a HF radio at the Office of the North West and Kununurra became a reporting station, the function which was carried out until the 1990's. In the early days, due to lack of general communications, HF radio became a sought-after backup and was constantly used for emergencies and urgent orders for things such as medicines.

The SES relied on the public and Government Departments to assist with manpower and resources to carry out operations which, at times, were many and varied. The most traumatic operation was providing reception facilities for both air and road evacuees following Cyclone Tracy in December 1974.

As the Kimberley became more developed in the 1990's and in response to increasing tourism in the region, local membership was sought and, with population increase, the Kununurra SES Unit was formed. Training programmes provided by FESA\DFES enabled SES members to carry out complex and technical operations, some requiring a great deal of expertise.

Searches for aircraft, land searches for persons, some of which still remain a mystery to the present, searches for periods up to 7 days, marine accidents off the coast, location of and containment of "boat people", problems on lakes and rivers, Wet season problems such as flooding, road closures, stranded travellers, community evacuation and community re-supply etc, are some of the operations that the Kununurra SES became involved with.

The Kununurra SES Unit Volunteers respond to incidents across the region. Their capability includes a well trained and equipped vertical rescue team, land search teams, air observers, flood Boat operators, radio operators, chainsaw operators and storm damage response teams.

Locations of the SES have varied over the years from sheds to offices to a private home, though the unit had an allocation of land for a future building when funding could be found. The locations include Agate lane until it was no longer suitable and a new location was identified at the current location in Coolibah Drive where a purpose built co-location facility was developed for Fire and Emergency Service vehicles, boats, state of the art training areas and an air conditioned emergency operations centre, radio room, administration office and kitchen.

Major incidents and significant events involving the Kununurra Unit of the SES include:

- Active engagement with ADF during Kangaroo 89 and 91 exercises.
- Search and containment of "boat people".
- Drop master assistance to upturned barge in Sir Joseph Bonaparte Gulf.
- Vertical Rescue assistance at Lennard Gorge, Amalia Gorge El-Questro and Andy's Chasm.
- Land searches – Balgo, Manning Gorge, Mitchell Plateau\Surveyors Pool, Bungle Bungles (Purnululu National Park).
- Air searches Canning Stock route, Kimberley coast.
- Evacuation of Oombulgurri Aboriginal Community.
- First assistance to Kalumburu after severe tropical cyclones Iver, Steve and Ingrid.
- First response Warmun flooding disaster, 2011.
- Communications assistance during West Kimberley Fires.
- Support to Bushfires Brigades during bushfires.
- Support for many unfortunate drowning and suicides in the Ord River.
- Several resupply incidents during floods.

The Kununurra SES Local Coordinator/Manager from 1989 to 1996 was John Hobbs. Richard Watkins was the Local Manager from 1996 to 1998. Lincoln Heading took over the role as Local Manager in 1998 and served 22 years before handing over to the current Local Manager, Scott Jenkins, in January 2020.

Mandurah State Emergency Service Unit

Historically, it is unique that the Mandurah State Emergency Service was initially founded by the Reverend Father Franz Edward Hope, a local Catholic parish priest, after a small boy was trapped down a borehole in Mandurah in January 1957. Volunteers worked non-stop before a satisfactory rescue was made after 23 hours had passed.

Prior to this, the town of Mandurah, with a population of 12,000 and a summer population of 25,000, had no rescue services, the nearest being at Pinjarra. The town was again rocked by a drowning tragedy shortly after in 1959 when another Catholic priest and three nuns lost their lives in a boating accident.

In 1975, after leadership was handed over to Fred Booker, the members' numbers and interests began to grow. The Mandurah shire council gave the group permission to erect a 30ft x 30ft iron-framed shed on council property in Park Road, as a base for training, storage, and operations, including the "Local Emergency Operations Centre" (LEOC). The new building was officially opened by the then Shire President, Cr. Pat Thomas. With the retirement of Mr Booker, the unit continued to grow in credibility and strength, with leadership coming from Geoff Burrell, followed by Barry Bell, until 1985 when Neil Davidson was appointed as Local Co-ordinator by the Mandurah Shire Council

In 1988 with the town's population approaching city status, plus the continued high membership of the group, it was imperative that a feasibility study of the existing premises be reviewed for the expansion of the LEOC to meet requirements under the Mandurah Counter Disaster Plan. The building upgrade's urgency was fully realized in August 1988 when the town was devastated by a tornado, causing extensive damage to approximately 100 dwellings and collateral damage.

The aftermath of the tornado resulted in an immediate fundraising activity to rebuild the LEOC and accommodate the rescue services and the Mandurah Counter Disaster Committee when the disaster occurred. The council partly funded the upgraded Mandurah LEOC with the balance coming from donations and sponsorship. Added to this was 5,000 hours of volunteered labour, freely given by members in various ways during construction. The new building was officially opened by the Mayor of the

City of Mandurah, Bruce Cresswell, on the 7th April 1990. In addition to the building project, the members of the Mandurah Unit, by their endeavours over several years, have accrued and extensive range rescue equipment.

There are eight long serving members who have been recognised for their distinguished service and awarded the Emergency Services Medal (ESM) under the Australian Honours and Award system.

Local Manager Neil Davidson OAM CD became the longest-serving manager of the Mandurah SES until he passed away following an illness in 2010. His dedication to community service and continued growth of the Mandurah SES was an inspiration to many. Mr Christopher Stickland ESM, was appointed as the Local Manager in late 2010. The Mandurah SES is now well placed with the numbers and quality of its Volunteers to serve the community in times of need or disaster.

Marble Bar State Emergency Service Unit (now a VFES Unit)

An article written at the end of the 80s or very early 90s by a Marble SES Volunteer.

"An SES Unit has again been established in Marble Bar. This was the result of a public meeting called Marble Bar recently to discuss the lack of emergency services.

With no Volunteer Fire Brigade, St John Ambulance or SES in the town, the OIC of Marble Bar Police Senior Constable John Yates told the meeting he could only call on "amateurs to lend a hand" in an emergency situation.

It was resolved the most appropriate organization to handle any emergency was the SES and among the first to join was Rob Emilliani and Alf and Olga Potter. These members were very active in 1980-81 and undertook a number of Training exercises before interest in the unit declined.

Since the unit has been reformed, members Steve McGillivray and Peter Barker have attended a Basic Mass Rescue Course in Port Hedland and Wyn Cook attended a local Coordinators course in Perth.

On the weekend of 9-10 July, the Marble Bar SES Unit played host to seven Volunteers from the Newman SES Unit and seven from the Port Hedland SES Unit for a Map Reading Course. On 30-31 July, Marble Bar SES will again play host to a First Aid course at which members from other units will be invited to attend.

A special thanks to WASES Regional Co-ordinator Ian Rector and Tracy Dunn for their efforts in organising these courses and also to the Volunteer instructors – some have to travel 600km to the "Bar" to conduct the course.

It is also a measure of the enthusiasm in the Newman SES Unit when it is remembered they have to travel 300km on dirt roads to attend."

Margaret River State Emergency Service Unit

As documented by John Alferink, long serving volunteer from 1975 to 2008:

"My first recording of an emergency service agency in the Margaret River town was that Mr W.H Samworth was made head warden of Civil Defence in 1942.

In 1961 the organisation was changed to the State Emergency Service. I also remember the service being called the VES (Volunteer Emergency Service).

The Shire had a building on the corner of Bussell Highway and Churchill St operating for storage of welfare equipment until the newly formed Moondyne Arts and Crafts took it over for their craft room in 1974.

When I joined in 1975 the SES was under Shire control with the then Shire Clerk John Reidycrofts the co-ordinator. Some of the members were Kevin Waddington, Rex and Betty Dyer, Barbara Taylor, Rob Barnett, Keith Tritton and Ben Malpass.

We operated out of a storeroom located behind the Shire building. Some of the equipment we had were flood boat, troop carrier landcruiser, catering equipment and WW2 stretchers. The landcruiser was shared with the Shire for ranger patrol and bushfire duties.

We joined with the other units for training, competitions the then regional co-ordinator was Duncan Glendinning. My first real callout was when the Blackwood River flooded in January 1982. It caused the old Alexandra Bridge to be broken up. Peter Wood and I had the job to watch the old bridge which had been under stress with all the various logs against it. It was thought that the old bridge when broken would float downstream and collide with the new bridge. At the height of the flood we saw the old bridge give way but the fear of collision did not eventuate.

The training, and competition with other units continued under the then Shire Clerk Ken Preston.

After the retirement of Duncan Glendinning in 1982 Nial Wilmott took over as Regional Manager and he set about making all the units ship shape in the South West.

In July 1986 the first Augusta whale rescue stretched our resources to the limit with many members being involved including Richard Leather and Kim Carver. We helped firstly with the whale transfer from Colourpatch beach to Flinders Bay then with the welfare of the numerous volunteers who had been in the water for many hours and were at risk of hypothermia. The whale and dolphin strandings in 1988 and 1989 were also attended by our unit, more in a welfare and crowd control assistance.

The SES also carried out general crowd assistance at the Leeuwin Concerts since 1986 and that continued to the present day. Other concerts at Ellenbrook and Vasse Felix were also attended in more of a car parking duties.

In 1989 the then Shire Clerk Ken Preston relinquished his position as co-ordinator and former Shire President John Yates took over. Through his efforts the former Telecom lineyards in Le Souef St were acquired and the unit very much appreciated the space, access, buildings compared to what we were in before. From there, the unit grew rapidly with many new recruits in Beryl Anderson, Lyn McMaster, Nathan Darch, Frank Yates, Pam Yates, Bob Castle, Raylene Castle, Helen Clements, John Anderson, Thelma Cooley, John McMaster, Paul Dyer, Chris Smith, Joe O'Conner, Ian Porter, Gail Walley, Allan Walley, Peter Brockman and Glen Bradshaw.

The Margaret River Surf competition was fully controlled by the unit for a number of years however the great responsibility and time taken was too demanding, so it was discontinued. The funds raised from these events was a great help for the purchase of new equipment and later renovations to our new headquarters.

The unit was involved in a number of searches for missing people who were gratefully found. The search for a crashed aircraft in Osmington, which led to the discovery of two bodies was a great shock to some members. The counselling which was later available to the members involved in the rescue at the Gracetown cliff collapse would have been of great help then.

The unit has been involved with many other emergencies such as storm damage, flooding, in our shire and also neighbouring shires.

When John Yates retired, his position was taken on by Joseph O'Conner however he resigned after a short while and Frank Yates took on the role. He was ably assisted by his wife Pam and she was rightly awarded the Peter Keller award for outstanding service to the unit. Other members to receive awards with National medals were John Yates, Frank Yates, Kim Carver and John Alferink.

In 1999, the SES, Fire Services and Bush Fire Board formed the Fire and Emergency Services Authority, FESA. They were later joined by Sea Search and Rescue and the Emergency Services Cadets.

Nial Wilmott retired as the South West Regional Manager in 2001 and his replacement was Paul Carr. Newer members to join the unit were Paul McKenzie, Lynda Burch, Melynda Burch, Carissa George, Leonie George, Jan Palmer-Vaughan, Jacki Lotan, Susan Doye, Ian Lee, Natasha White, Brad Burch, Amanda Stolley, Paul Walton, Melinda House, Fred Morrison, Mick Harknett, Wendy Harknett, Kelena Beale, Ross Duits, Troy Burch, Robbie Gratten-Wilson, Anthony Gratten-Wilson.

Frank Yates retired as unit manager in 2006 and he was replaced for a short while by Ian Lee until Lynda Burch took over and is still in charge now (in 2008).

I also retired in 2006 after a great 31 years of unit comradery, successful searches, storm damage repairs and public appreciation.

It was great to see that one of our very dedicated members Paul Lieper was made South West District Manager in 2008."

The first Margaret River emergency agency was established as the Civil Defence Unit in 1942. The Units name was changed to Volunteer Emergency Service (VES) occupying a Shire Building on the corner of Bussell Highway and Churchill St in 1961.

In 1974 the unit relocated to a storeroom behind the Shire building, operating under Shire control. The Unit changed its name again to the Busselton State Emergency Service during the early 1980s and relocated to the formed Telecom Lineyards in Le Souef St in 1989. In 2007 the Unit name changed again when the Augusta-Margaret River SES became incorporated as a Not-for-Profit organisation.

The region name changed in 2012 with the creation of a new DFES District, the Lower South West District, following the split away from the South West District and the Units new facilities were opening in the same year between Clarke Rd and Railway Terrace.

The Margaret River Unit Co-ordinators between 1975 and 1989 included former Shire Clerks John Reidycrofts and Ken Preston. Local Managers (Co-ordinators) from 1989 were Joseph O'Conner for a short time, then John Yates who handed over to long serving Local Manager Frank Yates until 2006. Ian Lee held the position for a short time before Lynda Burch took on the role for the next 6 years. Lisa Hosking taking over in 2012, followed by Lewis Hawkins in 2015 until handing over in 2018 to current Local Manager Adrian Yates

Meekatharra State Emergency Service Unit

An article written in the early 2000s by inaugural Local Co-ordinator Keith D. Mouritz:

"In 1988 a meeting was held in the Sporting Complex in Meekatharra. It was presided over by Regional Co-ordinator Bernie McNamara, representing the WASES. It was called by a gentleman who was employed by the Civil Aviation Authority as a Flight Service Officer at the Meekatharra airport. He apparently had attended a Local Co-ordinators course in Victoria. Those present included representatives of Shire, Government Agencies, and various mines and service organisations. I intimated I could possibly call for members for a unit from my associates in the Buffaloes Lodge. I was asked later on if I could see my way clear to attend a Local Co-ordinator course in Perth. I approached the Shire and they agreed that I attend and subsequently did so.

After being enlisted in the SES I, in turn, enlisted a group of people to the Unit.

We were originally attached to Carnarvon under Ross Holmes and Allen Gale management. Later being transferred to Geraldton.

My son Noel and myself travelled to Carnarvon and picked up various articles of equipment, overalls etc.

As the girls change room wasn't being used (at the Meekatharra Oval Sports Centre), I confiscated it to store the equipment. After visits from Instructors we eventually became a viable unit.

I continued as Local Coordinator/Manager for some years and attended several incidents, as required.

I passed over the management of the Unit to Ron Hiscock, who on resigning that job, the Local Manager job was taken on by Roy Seery. He in turn was followed by Robyn Morris as Local Manager. On her retirement the appointment of Dennis Shaw was approved by Regional Manager as Local Manager and he still enjoys that position.

I still hold the position of Unit Treasurer which I thoroughly enjoy."

A purpose-built Unit Headquarters was constructed by the shire in the mid-1990s.

The Meekatharra SES Unit has participated in Land searches for missing persons and done a lot of sandbagging and plastic covering of roofs after rain and windstorms, including a severe hailstorm in the early 1990's that punched holes in about 40 buildings in Meekatharra.

Melville State Emergency Service Unit

An article written by former volunteer Tom B. Joyce who joined the Melville Civil Defence and Emergency Service Unit in 1975:

"Early 1973 I made contact with the then Controller of the Melville Civil Defence and Emergency Service Group, Mr R.F. Fleahy.

After exchanging correspondence with Mr Fleahy during 1973 and 1974, with a view to joining the group, nothing eventuated.

Enquiries at the Melville City Council, regarding re-activation a Civil Defence Unit, which at this time appeared to have faded out, the town Clerk advised me that it was my prerogative to do something it I wished.

During 1975 the Melville Council were advised that a training course was coming up at Mt Macedon in Victoria.

An employee of the council was nominated to attend this course, which was for a "Rescue Instructor". This person nominated was not interested in attending as he knew that I was, advised me of his intention to decline the offer.

After discussions with the Town Clerk I was nominated to attend the "Rescue Instructors" Course at the Counter Disaster College.

At this time the initials "C.D." were known generally as Civil Defence but these were now being used to mean "Counter Disaster".

After completing the course and being qualified as a "Rescue Instructor", the next move was to organize a group of volunteers and become an active unit.

Being a member of the Four-Wheel Drive Club of WA at this time I called for volunteers at a four wheel drive club meeting and immediately received nominations from 19 very keen club members who were eager to learn new skills and rescue techniques.

As an employee of the Melville City Council, I was given the use of the "old" Melville Road Board building located at the intersection of Canning Highway and Stock Road in Palmyra, a suburb of Melville, to use for meetings and general training.

This old building was quite dilapidated and run down, but cleaned up OK, and it did include the original lock-up strong room which was ideal as a storage area. The strong room and council room had in fact been used by the now defunct Civil Defence Group and did contain small amount of equipment, such as a few ex-army folding stretchers, bits and pieces of 1st aid kits, some military style leather boots and gaiters, a few pairs of blue, ex-air force overalls and some old torches.

Radio communications were very poor from this location and it was necessary at times to drive or walk cross the road to a better location to improve this problem. There were odd occasions when it was necessary to travel down the road a short distance and use the Palmyra Police facilities."

Significant incidents include:

- May 1994 storms when the unit attended over 150 residences in the local area and were operational for 36 hours.
- 1998 when a cattle truck resulted in a cow escaping into the Piney Lakes and remaining free for some months. An SES search team from Melville, the SES Mounted Section on horses and the stock

- horses from the Livestock company tracked, chased and finally drove her out of her cover and she was lassoed rodeo style.
- 1999 when a tornado struck East Fremantle tearing a roof off a 10-story block of flats in East Street. At the same time the unit attended 60 other residences from East Fremantle to Tompkins Park; all effected by the same storm.
- May 2005 a tornado crossed the Swan River in Bicton destroying a primary school classroom; luckily it was about an hour before children were due to arrive at the school. Many homes also suffered roof damage with the unit attending to them at the time and also revisiting many of them for months to fix temporary repairs due to the lack of builders available to carry out repairs straight away.
- March 2010 Perth hailstorm saw the unit adapt to a Regional Control Centre as the Belmont "Bunker" suffered damage. The unit was operational for more than 72 hours.

Today to Unit operates from modern facilities co-located with City of Melville Operations Centre, built in 2001.

Local Controllers/Co-ordinators include Doug Anderson and Tom Joyce between 1976 and 1994. Local Manager Kevin Wrightson is the longest serving having commenced in 1994 – and handing over in 2007 to Robyn Trainer. David Fyfe served in the role from 2013 – 2016. The current Local Manager is Andrew Treen.

Mount Barker State Emergency Service Unit

The Mount Barker SES has been proudly serving the community for almost 50 years. A commemorative plaque hangs on the wall of our Unit acknowledging its presentation to our predecessors in 1974, the Mount Barker Volunteer Emergency Service Unit.

The Ormond Rd site has a house and shed that the SES use for training and for storing equipment. Before the SES occupied the site, the shed was likely used for storage and loading trucks during WWII. A tactical map of the probable strike locations across Mount Barker is still pined to a wall in the house.

On Thursday night training, volunteers from across the Great Southern Units used to practice communications protocols through radio contact with each other. This piece of SES training history has fallen through since the other Great Southern Units have stopped Thursday night training, but the Mount Barker SES have proudly stayed with this training slot.

On the 1997 Competitions Day the Mount Barker SES where awarded a trophy for best first aid/rescue.

At one time Mount Barker SES had a vertical rescue role but it was surrendered due to lack of qualified team members.

The Unit has had several managers over the years. In 2008 Local Manager Ian Foote purchased each of the members a small thank you gift presented at the Christmas dinner, but it was temporarily discontinued. Current Manager Kirsten Beidatsch implemented a similar award on an annual basis.

In 2015, Kirsten Beidatsch won the SES Youth Achievement Award. She started her term in 2014 and is the youngest female manager to ever lead the Mount Barker SES.

The Mount Barker SES has always shared a good relationship with other volunteer organisations in the region. Since 2019 the Unit has participated in several cross-organisation training and rescue operations, with St John Ambulance, local Rangers, and advanced forensics training with the Mount Barker Police.

The Unit also houses the State-Wide Storm Cache Regional Detachment in the shed. The Storm Cache has been kept in the shed for over 7 years but was expanded and improved to the Regional Detachment in 2019. The Detachment was deployed to the Albany SES Unit to combat a severe flooding incident that inundated the town in August 2020.

In our time serving the community, Mount Barker SES have participated in the search and rescue of many people from the Stirling Ranges to the Albany Gap. In December 2019, half of the volunteers missed the Unit Christmas Party because they were searching for a missing person in the Stirling Range National Park, who was fortunately found alive and well a few days later.

Further to this in 2019, Mount Barker SES were instrumental in recovering two fatalities from the base of Bluff Knoll in the Stirling Ranges. It is always sad when a search ends in a fatality but at least we were able to bring closure to their families.

Mundaring State Emergency Service Unit

The Mundaring State Emergency Service was established in 1990. Like many SES units there was a need relating to response to natural hazard events in the local community

The Units first headquarters was located in the vacant Hillston Boys Correctional facility in Stoneville and then was moved to Burra St in Mundaring's industrial area.

In 2007 the new headquarters were opened at the current location where it is co-located with Mundaring Volunteer Fire & Rescue Service and the Darling Range Bush Fire Communications Brigade (Incident Control Vehicle).

The Mundaring SES Unit operates on the urban/rural fringe where it can operate either in residential parts of the metropolitan area or in rural areas. It also covers extensive areas of National Parks where the Unit is often part of a first response for missing persons. The Unit also provides support to 12 bush fire brigades within the Mundaring Shire with transport for responders and equipment, a lighting tower and any other infrastructure required to respond to these types of Natural hazards.

The inaugural Local Co-ordinator in 1990 until 1992 was Cornelius de Bruin von Gelderm, followed by Karl Mucjanco until 1997. Local Managers to follow included Jim Archibald until 2003, Lin Booth until 2010, Robbie Palmer until 2016 and currently Hendrik Raak.

Newman State Emergency Service Unit

The Newman SES Unit was established in July 1981 around the same year that the Shire of East Pilbara (SoEP) took management of the Town from Mt Newman Mining, whom established the town (originally Mount Newman) in 1966 as a closed Mining company town.

The Unit initially operated from a site provided by a local contractor until 1984. Then the SoEP secured funding to build a new shed for SES use at the Shire Depot in Woodstock St, Newman. During 1995 the Unit moved to the current location Lot 300 Kurra St which is SoEP owned where the SES utilised existing buildings for their administration and headquarters purposes. In 2004 the Unit added an equipment shed to the Kurra St facility.

By 2005 the Newman SES Administration Building on Kurra St was considered no longer fit for purpose for SES operations and was replaced. Due to its remote location, Newman was identified as a location requiring the capacity to operate as a Level 2/3 Incident Control Centre providing DFES with a facility from which to manage incidents where the Department of Fire and Emergency Services is the HMA within the East Pilbara Shire area and the Northern part of the Shire of Meekatharra.

The new facilities in Kurra St were officially opened on the 1st June, 2018 by the Minister for Emergency Services, Fran Logan MLA, and FES Commissioner Darren Klemm ASFM, enhancing the Newman SES function and profile within the East Pilbara Shire.

A key strength of the Newman SES is that they are very focussed on Prevention and Preparedness within Remote Aboriginal Communities. Each year the Unit spends a week travelling approximately 2,500kms visiting remote communities before the cyclone/wet season, maintaining a working relationship that has significantly reduced the need for resupplies - due to the effect of isolation each year within the East Pilbara Shire.

Current Local Manager Connie Reed is one of the longest serving Newman SES Volunteers.

Northam District State Emergency Service Unit

The Northam District State Emergency Service was established as a Civil Defence and Emergency Service unit in the 1960s with some allocated equipment stored in a room at the old Northam railway station after it closed in 1966.

District forms part of the name of the unit because the Volunteers of the Northam District SES have always covered several local government areas, including the Shire of Cunderdin where members from Northam responded to Meckering following the earthquake in 1968.

The subsequent earthquake preparations resulted in several members being trained at Mount Macedon in Victoria as instructors in disaster rescue, disaster welfare and disaster communications.

Northam is a significant town in the Avon Valley that is historically impacted by major riverine flooding due to it being sited at the convergence of two rivers. When the Mortlock is in flood it causes the Avon to bank-up and flood hundreds of homes and businesses that were built in the flood plain decades earlier.

A purpose-built headquarters was constructed in the Northam Showgrounds in 1979 where the newly formed Northam Local Volunteer Emergency Service (NLVES) Rescue Team held its first meeting in February 1980. Three years later the Swan Brewery Shield was presented to the NLVES Rescue Team when they won the last State Emergency Service Week - Rescue Competition held at Gloucester Park. The shield still adorns the wall of the headquarters along with many other awards and proud memorabilia.

The Volunteers raised considerable funds through the 1990s to carryout major extensions to the headquarters and construct a large garage to store vehicles and equipment. In 2020 the Central Brigade of the Northam Shire's Bushfire Service co-located with NDSES at their headquarters where they have been based for 40 years.

The Civil Defence and Emergency Service Controllers of the 1960s and 70s were Jim Payne and Bill Archer. The SES Local Coordinators of the 1980s and early 1990s were Sonny Raymond, Richard Grigson (twice) and Allen Gale. The SES Local Managers through the 1990s to 2020 have included Silvia Bristow-Stagg, Tony Dowe, Julie Brown, Sergio Bottacin and currently Cheryl Greenough since October 2019.

There have been many Volunteers passing through this unit with some of those taking on major roles within WASES/FESA/DFES including Allen Gale and Greg Cook (District Managers).

Northshore State Emergency Service Unit

(Perth SES and Subiaco SES merged 1996, Nedlands SES disbanded early 1980s)

The Northshore State Emergency Service Unit was established nearly 50 years ago, starting out life as the Perth SES unit, and later merging with the Subiaco SES Unit. There was no plan – when storms hit the city, half a dozen Perth Council Officers donned their blue overalls and drove around the local street in their council vehicles responding to requests from the then assistant city engineer, who was also driving around in his vehicle spotting problems. Shortly after this inaugural event, a truck, two rescue trailers and equipment were supplied by the Perth Council, and following completion of a rescue leader's course at Mt Macedon, Victoria in 1973, Ian Lush became the first Controller of the Perth SES unit.

In mid-1974 the City of Perth SES unit was formed. Ian Lush was the Acting Local Coordinator although the Deputy Town Clerk was the nominated Local Co-ordinator. The Unit was originally referred to as the Volunteer Civil Emergency Service (VCES) and not long thereafter as the Perth Civil Emergency Service (PCES), before transitioning to the Perth State Emergency Service Unit.

Originally, all volunteers within the Perth SES unit were council employees, primarily because the Emergency Operations Centre (EOC) and equipment storage facilities were within the secure council depot where the Perth Unit originally met at 226 James Street, Northbridge. It included a small storage room on the west side of the depot, where we kept our (meagre) equipment, ropes, etc and the Board Room on the 1st floor that had been modified to use as an Emergency Operations Centre (EOC), complete with extra phones and a cache of forms, paper, pencils, etc. An aerial had been installed on the roof and wired to the Board Room, so that we could use a radio Base station.

The original Perth SES unit solely served the City of Perth and had two vehicles (a 1973 International D1100 van and a 1993 4x4 Ford Maverick which it shared with the Building Department) and operated from the Council depot in James Street.

The Perth SES was the first SES Unit to qualify in Single Rope Techniques. The rationale was that, in the event of an earthquake, damaged masonry and rubble were likely to clog up the stairwells in the high rise buildings, so it was considered appropriate for the rescuers to be able to get to the roof of the building and abseil down to a window. At that time every floor had to have a minimum of 1 opening window so access could be gained to upper floors by abseiling down and entering the window.

In 1989 the unit moved to a former City of Perth day care centre at 60 Tower St (later renamed Frame Court), Leederville. This allowed for a significant change in that recruitment of volunteers could now include non-council employees, as the EOC was no longer located within a secure area.

May 1994 saw Perth and the South West battered by severe storms, with wind gusts up to 140kmph. Significant damage was caused to move then 600 homes, with widespread power outages lasting more than 7 days and many parts of Perth and the Western Suburbs were inundated under huge tides and large swell.

In 1996 the breakup of the City of Perth into four local governments and the creation of the new Towns of Cambridge, Vincent and Victoria Park, meant that these local governments had no formal arrangements for the provision of emergency services.

The name "Northshore" was conceived by the then WASES Regional Manager Jim Burnett during a review to provide a more comprehensive service model. This led to the creation of the new SES Unit titled the Northshore State Emergency Service Unit and resulted in an amalgamation of the former Perth and Subiaco State Emergency Service unit personnel, vehicles and equipment.

The review also resulted in the new SES Unit being funded by nine member Councils: City of Perth, City of Vincent, Town of Cambridge, City of Subiaco, City of Nedlands, Town of Claremont, Town of Cottesloe, Shire of Peppermint Grove and Town of Mosman Park. With the introduction of the ESL the SES funding grant application and acquittal process has been managed by the Town of Vincent.

The March 2010 Hailstorms resulted in a total of 844 Requests for Assistance from residents and ratepayers in the Northshore area. The Unit was operational for a total of 9 days and, at one period 17 teams were operating in the area. The operation was co-ordinated by Jim MacLean with relief assistance being provided by James Hines.

Nowadays, the Northshore SES unit has a volunteer membership of about 60 trained to be able to deal with whatever emergency situation may confront them, as well as many other support & miscellaneous roles, and despite being a member of one particular unit, the volunteers may be deployed anywhere in Australia at any time.

There is no such thing as a typical callout for any SES unit. However, the more common types of incidents for Northshore include searching for missing persons, storm damage, and buildings damaged by vehicle impacts.

Northshore SES finally moved to 3-7 Lynton St, Mt Hawthorn in June 1999. The site had been established as the SES Metropolitan Region office in April

1978, with the Metropolitan Regional Office moving to Leake St, Belmont in 1999.

In 1997 Ian Lush was officially appointed as Local Manager of Northshore SES. The position of Local Co-ordinator for the Perth SES unit was traditionally held by a senior Council Officer, such as the Director Engineering Services. However, the co-ordination of the Unit since 1974 was actually carried out by Ian Lush. Ian retired after 43 years handing over the reins to long time Deputy Manager Jim McLean, who in turn handed over the reins to Deputy Manager Nick Elliott who is the current Local Manager since 2011.

Pingelly State Emergency Service Unit

In 1984 as a result of a fatal road accident west of Pingelly and the inability to be able to release the victim from the wreckage, a public meeting was convened. As a result of the meeting funds were raised to set up a Road Rescue Trailer and equipment within the town of Pingelly. There was a need for Volunteers to train and respond to road accidents with this trailer. This was the beginning of the Pingelly State Emergency Service Unit.

The Road Accident Rescue (RAR) equipment was tested out at an incident in 1985 and since then has attended on an average of 6 road accidents a year from minor injuries to fatal incidents. The longest RAR task took 2 hours to release the trapped person who, after 3 weeks confined to hospital, returned to employment completely recovered from the ordeal.

The unit was issued with its first vehicle in March 1988 and this was a significant step as prior to this date the RAR trailer was towed by private vehicle. The Unit has been seen to be a high-profile Unit throughout the Great Southern region and the Unit members are very proud of their achievements.

Over the years the Unit has been successful in purchasing of new equipment, including a lighting tower. The Unit headquarters building has been extended and refurbished with a swing pole tower for communications and a training tower added from funds raised.

The Unit members were selected to participate in the National Road Crash Rescue Competition conducted by the Australasian Road Rescue

Organisation and were heavily involved with both Western Rescue competitions held in WA in the early 2000s.

The first Local Co-ordinator was Bunt Whiting for 6 months, followed by David Ford for a period of 12 months, then Rex Peters 8 months and the current Local Manager is Bill Mulroney ESM who was appointed as the Local Co-ordinator in 1986.

Rockingham-Kwinana State Emergency Service Unit

The Rockingham-Kwinana Emergency Service was formed in the mid 1970's following a number of storm events that impacted Rockingham as the need was identified from emergency service unit to assist the community.

In 1977 the Unit was known as the Rockingham Voluntary Emergency Service unit and changed soon after to the Rockingham State Emergency Service Unit. In 1990 the Town of Kwinana was included, and the name changed to the Rockingham- Kwinana State Emergency Service Unit.

The Rockingham-Kwinana SES respond to storm, flood, calls for assistance and support other services in the area for bush fire and car versus house events.

The Rockingham Kwinana SES volunteers have been deployed, not only in the metropolitan area or around the state of WA, but also to other states, including Queensland, Victoria and South Australia.

The Unit and its' volunteers have been involved in many operations, including a support role in 1986 for a 250lb unexploded bomb found in Warnbro, the May '94 storms and some major search operations in 1990 (Gabor Lavisi) and 1997 (Gerard Ross). The unit volunteers and also been deployed in major searches in Armadale and Morangup as requested.

In 1982 the Unit won the Rescue, Communications & Welfare components of the SES Week annual competition held at Nedlands.

The Rockingham Kwinana SES also had a tracker dog team until it was relocated in 2008. More than 20 SES members have received National medals.

The current complex housing the Rockingham Kwinana SES is located at Crocker Street Rockingham.

The Local Managers have included the first Local Co-ordinator, George Earnshaw from 1977 until 1987, followed by Michael Wadley OAM, Dave Beard and then Mark Wyatt. David Catchlove is currently acting in the role of Local Manager (2020).

There have been many Volunteers passing through this unit with some of those taking on major roles within FESA/DFES including Mike Wadley OAM (FESA District Manager), Gordon Hall ESM (FESA Director) and Grant Pipe (DFES Superintendent).

SES Canine State Emergency Service Unit

The Canine Unit started as the Canine Section in 2007. The forerunner was the Metropolitan Regional Tracker Dog Group that was based at the Metro Region headquarters from the 1980s until it was disbanded and the Volunteers along with their dogs and equipment joined the Rockingham-Kwinana SES Unit or the Stirling SES Unit.

Ian Spreckley was recruited by DO Darryl Ott to coordinate search dog training in the WA SES circa 2005. Ian is from England and is a retired multipurpose police dog handler and trainer and a volunteer area search dog handler, trainer and assessor.

As Subject Matter Expert and Training Coordinator, Ian introduced the United Kingdom National Search and Rescue Dog Association (NSARDA) standard of training and assessing for Air Scenting Area Search Dogs and Scent Specific Tracking Dogs.

The first operational search dog team to be qualified was a dog called Rhani and handler Francis Best.

In 2015 the Canine Section was gazetted as the Canine SES Unit which is a unit in the State Wide Operational Response Division (SWORD) of DFES and is deployed state wide.

The first Unit Manager was Leonie Briggs from 2015 until 2020 and the current manager is Rosemary Yeoh.

SES Communications Support Unit

The SES Communications Support Unit (CSU) was created around 1962 as a part of the Civil Defence and Emergency Service of Western Australia. It was the Communications Section of the State Headquarters. Volunteer members were known as Staff Officer Reserve (SOR) and were part of a group of Staff and Volunteers, along with Operations Section Volunteers, who managed State level operations for emergency incidents.

The group transitioned to being part of the Western Australian State Emergency Service when the Civil Defence part of the organisation's name was dropped in 1974. After the transition it retained its name of Communications Section. The group remained with these titles for about forty years until, in the early 2000s, it was formally approved as an SES Unit under the *FES act (1998)*. It then became the SES Communications Support Unit (CSU).

The CSU has continuously operated a volunteer Section/Unit to support the Western Australian community at State, Regional and Local levels and is not associated with specific local government boundaries. It is one of the longest operating SES groups in the State.

The CSU remains unique throughout Australia and has always included innovative volunteers serving their community and travelling throughout the State developing volunteers and staff in the establishment and maintenance of emergency communication systems.

During emergency operations, the CSU are regularly activated to establish and maintain critical communication links in areas where there is little or no existing radio and telephone services. In the earlier years the CSU specialised in HF, VHF and UHF radio and telephony systems and networks however, today the range of services provided extends to satellite communication, digital audio/visual data management over the Internet and dedicated secure channels.

As an SES Volunteer unit, the CSU has been managed by Volunteers, including Local Managers Cheryl Greenough, Stephen Summerton, Henry Edwards, Rob Crawford, Greg Cook and currently Chris Knight.

SES Mounted State Emergency Service Unit

Known almost always as the SES Mounted Section, the Unit is now a specialist group that, since 2014, falls under the umbrella of DFES SWORD (State-wide Operational Response Division).

The Unit was formed in 1987 as a subbranch of the Armadale SES Unit and after several years and searches became a regional resource and was taken over by Metropolitan Region in 1991.

In the early years the Units meetings were held in hotels and members houses while training took place at various venues, eventually moving its training venue in 2000 to the FESA-SES Metropolitan Regional Headquarters at 91 Leake Street Belmont.

In 2006 after considerable lobbying the Unit moved into its first real home in 12 Hehir Street Belmont. The facility was shared with the Belmont SES and was a temporary facility while a more permanent HQ for the two units was built. In 2012 the unit, along with Belmont SES moved into new HQ in Kew Street, Cloverdale. 2014 saw the Mounted Section incorporated into SWORD (State Wide Operational Response Division) and in 2017 the unit moved to new headquarters in Kewdale.

Over the years the Unit's profile has evolved from simply being a specialist search unit to include responsibility for management of the SES Animal Rescue Unit and the provision of operational support to Region and other units during hazards such as storms, cyclones, floods and fires.

The Local Coordinator/Manager include long serving member Dave Emery 1987-1990, then Helen Iles until 2003, followed by Stuart Jones until 2014 and currently Natalie Beard.

SES State-Wide Operational Response Division SWORD (Logistics) Unit

Original formation of the SWORD was born from the recommendations of the Fergusson Report into the Waroona/Yarloop Fires in which it was recognised that an additional, trained and available ready force be formed to bolster and be more successful than that which existed.

The initial SWORD firefighting capability sprang from the closing and amalgamation of the Bassendean and Guildford volunteer fire stations.

Other elements, such as logistics and Comms Support were identified as being an essential requirement due to the jurisdictional enormity of Western Australia which relies heavily on the volunteer support to provide the required capabilities at a financially viable level.

SWORD began life accommodated in a less than ideal shed/garage on Dundas Road High Wycombe adjacent to the DFES Academy. At the time there appeared to be no firm statement of role/function given to the then members who underwent the absolute basic SES Induction-type training – no real SES skills training at all.

February/March 2016 saw the start of planned skills training, based on the standard Local Government SES Unit function/roles. Since then, the Unit's role and functions have slowly developed into providing logistical support to the whole of the community of the State of Western Australia.

SWORD SES (Logistics) members have the unique opportunity to train in the normal SES type qualifications plus a variety of skills not being within the eAcademy, such as HR/MR driving, container knowledge, stores knowledge, dealing with trucks and driving, forklift driving, Hiab use, pallets and the like.

There has been a significant shift in the operational deployment timeline of SWORD in recent years. Traditionally, SWORD was deployed around 3-5 days into a major incident to provide redundancy and fatigue management options. With a huge increase in equipment capabilities and planned logistical responses across the State of Western Australia, the SWORD element is now routinely deployed at the very onset of a major incident and can remain deployed for period of up to approximately 9 days when deployed into the North of the state.

Currently housed in a leased warehouse facility on Ballantyne Road in Kewdale it is expected to re-locate in 2021 to larger and more suitable accommodation.

The SWORD SES (Logistics) Unit Managers include Derek Fletcher in 2015 and John White since 2016.

Shark Bay State Emergency Service Unit

The Shark Bay SES was established around 1983 firstly as a reporting station with a HF radio installed at the Shire Office in Denham. Weekly radio schedules were attended by Shire staff. The first storage shed was adjacent to the Shire Depot in Dampier Rd; however operations were always run out of the Denham Police Station or the Shire Office.

A new co-located headquarters with Volunteer Marine Rescue and St Johns Ambulance was opened 13th March 2015 situated in Durlacher St, Denham.

In the early part of the Unit's life, it was very active in vertical rescue area and members of the unit travelled widely through the north of the state passing on their skills and knowledge to members of other units, including Vertical Rescue (VR) Senior Instructor Steve Saunders. The unit VR activities were widely reported when members were involved in a rescue and recovery operation on Dirk Hartog island in 1989. Members travelled by boat to the eastern side of the island and then carried their VR equipment on foot across the Western side of the island to site of the boat wreck at the base of cliffs to rescue and recover personnel.

The Unit has provided searchers on land and in the air for countless searches for missing and overdue people both on land and at sea.

Local Co-ordinators/Managers include Shire Clerk at the time, Brett Pollock, followed by the Police OICs (S/c Steve Stingemore and S/c Mark Harring) for a few years then Dave Charles through the mid-90s, followed by Brian Veitch and currently Joe McLaughlin.

Stirling State Emergency Service Unit

The Stirling SES unit was formed in 1968 as a Civil Defence group with Joe Rice as Controller and Tom Appleyard as deputy. It is one of the oldest units in the metropolitan area and has been looking after the community for 52 years.

Stirling SES started at the back of the old City of Stirling Council building in Cedric St. There were two rooms, one for Communications and one for training. A lot of the training had to be conducted outside due to lack of space. There was a 2-bay shed that housed 2 vehicles, including an old Land Rover, and 3 rescue trailers. In the 1980s the unit was issued with a

Landcruiser which had to be garaged at the Local Coordinator, Maureen Grierson's house, again due to lack of space. When the council decided to demolish its Council building to rebuild the present council facility, Maureen secured the empty Nollamara Football Club building at 33 Carcoola Street, Nollamara and it was converted to suit the unit's headquarters needs in the 90s. The vehicles remained at the Cedric Street depot for a while in the 90s, so callouts were complicated, with a four-bay shed being built eventually on Sylvia Street. The Stirling SES is still located at Carcoola Street Nollamara with the Equipment Depot and Garage located around the corner in Sylvia Street which still presents a bit of a walk from the Unit headquarters.

Unit members have taken part in many Airborne searches, including the search for missing MH370 plane.

A specialist role Stirling SES held was Vertical Rescue with members conducting training at various locations. Some of the unit VR team members took part in the Karijini National Park Hancock Gorge rescue in 2004.

Another specialist role was Tracker Dogs. Brian Law was the leader of the SES Tracker Dog unit when the unit split from the Metro Region HQ with some members joining the Stirling SES and others joining Rockingham-Kwinana SES. Tracker Dog Teams ceased in 2007 when the Canine Unit was formed. There were many successful searches including the finding of a handgun. Dog training was undertaken at the unit along with taking part in search training out in the bush. Stirling lost its Canine status in 2010.

The unit enjoyed many years running the Kings Park area of Perth's Australia Day Skyworks, providing support for crowd control and even one year isolating a fire area when a firework set fire to the embankment.

Another role that was undertaken for many years was being part of the rescue teams at the Avon Decent. The trusty Land Rover carted canoeist and power boat participants who were injured or separated from their boats. It was a cold but fun at the overnight campsite for our SES unit volunteers.

The Local Coordinators/Managers include Joe Rice, Syd Rostron, Angus McKenzie, Glen Richards, Maureen Grierson, Simon Blears, Keith Squibb, Rick Guy, Jason Lansom (acting), Steven Perrie, Chris Hudson, Chris Brondsema, Doug Cooper and currently Greg Buck is Acting Local Manager.

Swan State Emergency Service Unit

The Swan State Emergency Service was originally an important part of the Civil Defence in Western Australia and was located at the back of the then Shire of Swan depot in Middle Swan.

The Volunteers of the Swan State Emergency Service cover a large local government area and have always been very active in Bush Fire Support as well as first responders during any of the major natural hazards in the area, in particular the effects of storms and localised flooding.

When other State Emergency Service units and local governments required assistance during emergency events, the Volunteers of the Swan State Emergency Service Unit are one of the first to respond and field the required teams, whether it is for storm damage, cyclone response and recovery or a large search. A number of the Swan SES Volunteers have been deployed to places such as Exmouth, Port Hedland and Broome.

The Local Managers have included Paul Shakes OAM, Les Hayter ESM, Tex McPherson ESM, Deb Bartlett, David Cowdell, Ashley Smith and Shaun Plummer.

There have been many Volunteers passing through this unit with some of those taking on major roles within FESA/DFES, Les Hayter ESM (Manager SES Training), Paul Shakes OAM, Tex McPherson ESM, Ashley Smith (District Managers), Shelly Staff (Administration) and Gordon Hall ESM (FESA Board member and FESA Director). The current complex housing the Swan SES was opened in 2012 and is located on Jack Mann Oval, Bishop Road, Middle Swan.

Toodyay State Emergency Service Unit

The Toodyay SES Unit is one of the newest Units and is co-located with the Morangup Bushfire Brigade on the western edge of Toodyay Shire in an impressive, recently renovated brick facility. The Unit is well equipped, having got off to a good start when a vehicle and equipment were transferred from Goomalling following the closure a few years early of an SES Unit.

The Local Manager is Jeff Venn.

Two Rocks State Emergency Service Unit

The Two Rocks SES Unit was formerly established in 2018 and is co-located with the Two Rocks Bushfire Brigade in a shared facility.

The Local Manager is Max Ross.

Useless Loop State Emergency Service Unit

The Unit kicked off in early 1989 with two volunteers, both of whom worked at Useless Loop, attending a Local Co-ordinators course at WASES State Headquarters.

They along with the salt mine operators were concerned with the response times to emergency incidents near the very difficult to access Steep Point.

Within a short time, the Unit developed a first response capability for Cliff Rescue, Road Crash Rescue and Land Search.

The Local Co-ordinators include the two volunteers who completed their LC course in 1989, Roy Tarpey and Bryan Cane. Local Managers include Darren Pepworth, Ainslea Hunt and Paul Berryman.

Wanneroo-Joondalup State Emergency Service Unit

The story began during a public meeting held by the Shire of Wanneroo on 25th July 1962. Concerns over fire control and Civil Defence led to the establishment of a Bush Fire Advisory Committee and Emergency Committee. In August 1962, the Emergency group consisted of Bill Mowart from St John Ambulance, Tony Martin from WA Police, Dr Reg Cox from the Shire, George Clover from the Forestry Department and a local resident, Murray Hamilton. This group went on to form 'The Wanneroo Civil Defence & Emergency Service', later renamed 'The Wanneroo Volunteer Emergency Service' (WVES) in 1975. At the time, the unit was located at the Wanneroo Showgrounds.

During the early 1980s, the name was changed to the State Emergency Service – Wanneroo Unit and the Unit was the overall winner of the 1983 State Emergency Service Week – Competition Day held at Gloucester Park.

The Unit relocated to 21 Winton Road Joondalup, where it remains today, in 1984. When constructed, the building consisted of an underground operations centre and three-bay vehicle shed. Over the years, another three vehicle bays were added to the shed to accommodate the growing fleet of vehicles. In 2013 four trailer bays were also added to protect the fleet of trailers from the elements.

In 2017 a second story was added to the underground Operations Centre. Giving us the area to operate as a Regional Operations Centre and ability to run multiple IMT's from the base.

The last name change occurred in 1998, when the City of Wanneroo split to form a second council, the City of Joondalup. Since this time, the Unit has been known as the Wanneroo-Joondalup State Emergency Service (WJSES).

The unit is fully equipped with an Isuzu crew cab truck (primary response vehicle), two Toyota land cruisers, one dual cab ute, two minibuses and a John Deere "side by side" utility vehicle. Other plant includes two mobile lighting plants, four bicycles, two storm damage trailers, a dedicated Vertical Rescue trailer and a Community Engagement trailer.

The Unit currently attends on average about 120 operational callouts per year. During recent history WJSES has had members involved in The Yanchep fires in 1991 & 2019, Moora Floods 1999 & the air search for Malaysian Airlines flight MH370 in March & April 2014. The Unit members have also been deployed to the north west on numerous occasions to assist with Cyclone damage & IMT duties. Members have been deployed to the eastern states for numerous incidents including, Victoria for storm damage 2010, NSW for IMT fire support 2002, Adelaide for storm damage 2016 & an air search from Cocos Island in 1991.

In 1998, a State Rescue Team was formed to compete in the National Rescue Skills Competition in Melbourne. WJSES had 3 members in this team which finished 2nd in the Competition.

The Local Co-ordinators/Managers over the years include Margaret Cockman 1971, David Lejeunne until 1973, John Inns until 1975, John Rucks until 1981, Ian Kelly until 1985, John Capes until 1991, Steve Foureur until 1995, Owen Peters until 1998, Graham Hodge until 2002, Andrew Stanbury until 2004, Geoff Watson until 2010, George Moylan until 2011, Bill Hansen until 2019 and currently Karina Saunders.

Boddington SES – circa 2002 (photo courtesy W English)

Rockingham SES – 2011 (photo courtesy D Price)

Kalamunda SES – 2010 (photo courtesy D Fletcher)

Mandurah SES – 2020 (Photo courtesy J Haslam)

Northshore SES - 2020

New Karratha SES Headquarters - 1988

Karratha SES Leadership Team at the opening of the new SES Headquarters (1988)

Karratha SES rescue vehicle and trailer – circa 1980s

SES Mounted section at Dowerin Field Day – circa 2003

SES Mounted section at a Mandurah public event - 2018

New Donnybrook SES Headquarters - 2014

New Gnowangerup SES Headquarters - 2016

Northam District SES State Competition Team – 1982

(courtesy Northam District SES)

New Belmont SES unit - 2013

Melville SES celebrating its 40th anniversary - 2016

Canine SES Search dog with Leonie Briggs - 2015

Wanneroo-Joondalup SES and Stirling SES Air Observers – 2011

(Photo courtesy D Brennen)

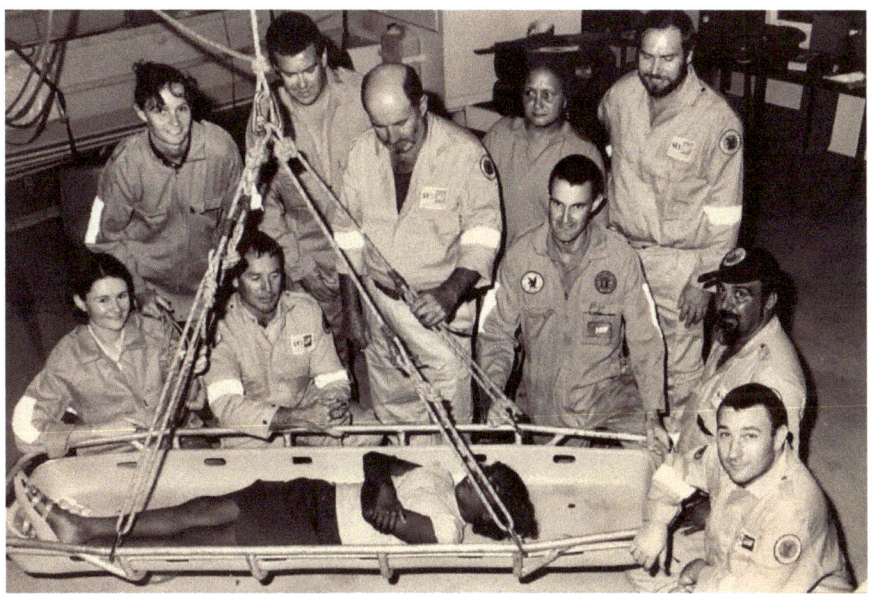

Kununurra SES training - circa 1998

CSU FOV 2019

CSU OKA training - circa 1989

Acknowledgements

It would not have been possible, without input from many Volunteers and Staff, past and present, to gather the information and compile it in an appropriate manner for this book.

For their assistance and help the author is very grateful.

Some of the Volunteers and Staff included;

John Capes OAM	Phillip Petersen ESM
Bernie McNamara ESM	Heather McNamara
Chris Widmer ESM	Nick Elrick ESM
Allen Gale	Adrian deKleer
Bill Mulroney ESM	Lin Booth
Mike Wadley OAM	George Sulc
Craig Chadwick	Michelle Hall
Jim Ridgwell	Connor Smith
Ivana Oroz-Bootsma	

The document has been peer reviewed by John Capes OAM and Allen Gale.

The proof reading was done by Kaye Lawry and Kerry Hall.

All their assistance and help is greatly appreciated.

The finalisation and production of this book would not have been possible without the support by the Minister for Emergency Services, the Hon Fran Logan MLA, and Commissioner Darren Klemm AFSM.

Biographies

Gordon M Hall ESM

Gordon's formal background is in Electronic Engineering however, he has always been involved in the community in many voluntary capacities, including as a District Governor for Apex, a charter President for a Lions club and the Chair of a School Council.

His Voluntary service in the SES started in 1993, at the Swan SES unit (WA) involving him in many searches and operations, including floods, storms and cyclone responses.

Gordon has been involved in the WA SES Volunteers Association since 1995 and has served as a Secretary and President, as well as an SES Consultative Committee representative.

Gordon was appointed to the first FESA Board representing the State Emergency Service. Later that year he was appointed as a Director with FESA and retired in 2011. During the period with FESA he was involved in many operations and was a key operative in the tsunami research and community preparation for Australia, as well as the resettlement of an indigenous nomadic group from Kiwirrkurra.

Currently he is a member of the Mandurah SES and serves as the Chair of the WA SES Volunteer Advisory Committee.

In 2018 the National SES Volunteers Association, a registered not for profit company, elected him as their Chair. This has given him the opportunity to pursue nationally the inclusion of young emerging leaders from SES, in national events and the promotion of women in the SES (his 40/40/20 rule).

Mr Hall's distinguished service was recognised when he was awarded the Emergency Services Medal in the Australia Day Honours list of 2018.

Allen J Gale ESM (Peer Reviewer)

Allen developed an interest in community self-help during his early scouting years and, after experiencing the staggering effects of the Meckering earthquake in 1968, joined the Northam Civil Defence and Emergency Service rescue team as a volunteer in 1970.

While Allen embarked on a road engineering drafting career with Main Roads, he also undertook many volunteer roles with the Northam District SES unit including that of Local Coordinator. This led him to a career within emergency services joining the WA State Emergency Service as a Training Officer in 1989.

Allen spent the next 10 years working with and developing SES volunteers and community-based organisations while based at Belmont, Carnarvon and Mount Hawthorn.

With the formation of FESA in 1999, Allen was appointed FESA District Manager SES Metropolitan North Region, moving to the role FESA District Officer, Media Liaison in 2005.

Allen completed a Master of Business Leadership (2007) from Curtin Graduate School of Business.

In 2013 he returned to DFES Operations Command as District Officer Operations Executive responsible for providing strategic advice concerning processes and change management for SES key stakeholders across the state. During this time he served as a DFES staff member on the WA SES Volunteers Advisory Committee.

Mr Gale retired from employment in April 2020 and his distinguished service was recognised in the Australia Day Honours list of 2021, where he was awarded the Emergency Services Medal.

John C Capes OAM (Peer reviewer)

John has a background in Electrical Engineering, and he was employed by the Commonwealth Government for 35 Years.

Following the impact of Tropical Cyclone Tracy on Darwin, John become interested in Emergency Services. It was in 1978 that he joined the Wanneroo Voluntary Emergency Service (later to become the Wanneroo SES).

John served in most leadership positions in the Unit and as the Local Coordinator (Local Manager) for six years which involved him in many operations at a Local, Regional and State Level.

John was always committed to representing Volunteers within the SES and was the driving force in establishing the first Volunteers Advisory Committee and then the now SES Volunteers Association.

John was appointed to the FESA Board in late 1999 as a member to represent the State Emergency Service. He remained in this role until the Board was abolished in September 2012.

John served several positions within the SESVA, including inaugural President, Vice President, Treasurer and now Editor and Webmaster.

John also has been awarded a National Medal and a DFES Service Medal for 35 years of Service.

Mr Capes's distinguished service with the WA SES was recognised when he was awarded the Medal of the Order of Australia in the Queen's Birthday Honours list of 2000.

www.ingramcontent.com/pod-product-compliance
Lightning Source LLC
Chambersburg PA
CBHW051536010526
44107CB00064B/2748